SHORTS

Also by Bill Reed

Plays
Burke's Company
Bullsh/ More Bullsh
Cass Butcher Bunting
Mr Siggie Morrison with his Comb and Paper
Truganinni
Living in Black Holes (anthology)
Living on Mars (anthology)
Living on Mars: the play
Daddy the 8th
Truganinni Inside Out
Auntie and the Girl
Mirror, Mirror
Little She
You Want It, Don't You, Billy?
The Pecking Order
Jack Charles is Up and Fighting
Just Out of Your Ground
I Don't Know What to Do with You!

novels
The Pipwink Papers\
Me, the Old Man
Stigmata
Ihe
Dogod
Crooks
Tusk
Throw her back
Are You Human?
Tasker Tusker Tasker
Awash
1001 Lankan Nights book 1
1001 Lankan Nights book 2
Passing Strange

Nonfiction
Water Workout

Award-winning short stories (see also title 'Passing Strange')
Messman on the C.E. Altar
The 200-year Old Feet
The Case Inside
Blind Freddie Among the Pickle Jars
The Old Ex-serviceman
The Shades of You my Dandenong

SHORTS

the short and one-act plays of

BILL REED

R

First published in 2016 by Reed Independent, Victoria, Australia.

Printed by Createspace.com, a division of Amazon.com.

Available as a printed book or an ebook from Createspace.com or
Amazon.com or Kindle estores, together with most major international online
outlets or bookshops with online ordering facilities:
paperback: ISBN 9780994630162
ebook: ISBN 9780994630179

Also available, either as this anthology or as the separate plays, via the
Australian Script Centre's website Australianplays.org

National Library of Australia Cataloguing-in-Publication entry:
Creator: Reed, Bill, author.
Title: Shorts/ Bill Reed
Edition: first
ISBN: 9780994630162 (paperback)
ISBN: 9780994630179 (ebook)
Notes: includes bibliographical references
Subjects: Drama anthology/one-act plays/short plays
Dewey Number: A822.3

Contents

Rocky

The Lizard of Oz

(one-act action and reaction)

The Lizard of Oz

She's called Tru, come from some hole down Old Truganinni Street.

He's called George Augustus R., sent by they-the-piper-pay back at the old Royal Society of Tassie to peg her down before she pegs out.

But who can lay down the real gen better than her old mate, Jessie, with her unique view from the bull bars of the Shag Magnet, that wheeliechair of wheelchairs?

This is two tattles of old Tru's tale.

Recorded and played out in one act, in which extinction is forever, give or take a day.

Setting

Evoked is an aged-care home in Melbourne.

Cast

TRU -- crusty Aboriginal senior. Never married, so did nix for her tribe's blood line anyway. Undoubtedly once a real stunner with her pert figure and plum-ripe face. Proudly busty; her back seems still braced. She would never have been kept quiet or quietened down. A worker all her life, mainly in the then Mission world of Tasmania where she was born, then as a kitchen hand at O'Lary Station, way up in the South Australian northlands and past a lot of shenanigans.

JESSIE – even crustier Scottish-born mate. An unwavering scrawniness such that her bones seem green twigs. Her eyes, though, are luscious and so easily filled with love. Whistle-talks with the dentures. When she strode off that migrant ship fifty years ago for marriage, she would have said, 'Rightio, who's game?'

GEORGE AUGUSTUS R. – sent by those-who-piper-pay back at head office of the Royal Society of Tassie to record TRU while they may. Life is a PowerPoint presentation in a pickle jar.

MANAGER -- has at least a projecting voice to his bluster, but that's about all.

The Lizard of Oz

(Lighting up as necessary to synch with GEORGE AUGUSTUS R.'s manual 'directorial' signals from front side, where he mainly remains throughout)

GEORGE AUGUSTUS R.: Don't blame me like for the rubbing out of the Tasmanian aborigines. I'm already treated like snot by they-who-the-piper-pay back at the office so it's no big surprise when they lumber me with recording these two old-boners down the old-boners home in Truganinni Street there, right? At least Nursie Nice-nough's nice enough to shunt me past the old near-goners watching the box in what could be the morgue been-in-come-out waiting room where old Tru and Jessie are hunched over the Sun-Herald's giant crossword like they wouldn't care if I'm from the United Nations' No Hope People Preservation Unit, so I'm recording straight off, aren't I? Get it? So, I guess, if you're like listening to what I'm getting down on memory here, old Tru's got the crotchety voice past gappy teeth and Jessie's the dentures with a chatty life of their own.

(TRU and JESSIE appear as he describes. He waits for them patiently before continuing:)

GEORGE AUGUSTUS R.: The time I'm getting all this, old Tru's blowing her grey mop over old Jessie's dumb silence over some clue or other and suddenly losing her nanna, screech-like going:

TRU: (furiously) What's the delay, what's the time lag?

GEORGE AUGUSTUS R.: … and Jessie's mistaking that as another clue altogether and having to clunk-clunk mentally think about that too then, before going back:

JESSIE: Time lag?

TRU: Time lag, time lag.

(pause)

JESSIE: How many letters?

GEORGE AUGUSTUS R.: …And then old Tru really blowing her stack this time:

TRU: Dopey old moll!

JESSIE: Who's a dopey old moll?!

TRU: You're a dopey old moll!

GEORGE AUGUSTUS R.: So, mostly at first, all I'm seeing is the old girls staring meet-me-around-the-back at each other. Some vital-you-get-it-down-quick assignment. I'm going, like, what are they-who-the-piper-pay using some lame oral-history excuse to get me out of the office, or something?... you know how you feeling-sorry-for-yourself go, like… when suddenly old Tru throws down her stubby pencil and pokes me in the belly button follow-me-bozo. She goes springing…
(he is actually narrating what the old ladies do…)
see?... to her feet with real surprising agility and has already started to trundle off down the long amber corridor there. You know what those corridors in those joints are like… the dawn-of-the-skate-boarder, like. And there's Jessie spurting out her own outrage at being left

behind. See her get-up-n'-go not far behind too! The trouble was she doesn't have the oil in the joints to overcome gravity as easily as Tru. When she finally gets a head of steam up, her Tru's already metres ahead and gaining headway. In outright panic now, Jessie shoves me out of the way and clambers to fall into line behind her Tru. Listen to the sound track; you can hear even me slipping'n'sliding, blowing my top trying to keep up. Tru was klaxoning ahead.

> *(And even though, as a train, they are literally slipping and careening around in a slow zig-zag:)*

TRU: (shout to nobody up-ahead) Watchit, mugs!

JESSIE: (from behind) Honk, shaggin' honk!
> *(but then bitchingly to TRU:)*
Hey, you stick to the shitty left!

TRU: ('whee') Up the shitty left!

JESSIE: Hey, you stick to the road rules!

TRU: Up the road rules!

> *(TRU finally 'reaches' what must be the end of the corridor, bounces off the opposite wall and then, doing a cartoony wheelie on one foot, turns the corner and is gone from sight, with JESSIE not too far behind now, and a triumphant from TRU:)*

TRU: Watch out, World! Madam Mountain coming through!

> *(Lighting 'blinks' on and off, and the old ladies are gone)*

7

GEORGE AUGUSTUS R.: So there was the three of us squishing and squelching on the old-bones near-goner lino. Hey, I was being paid for that, like? As I say, the things they-who-the-piper-pay lumber you with back at the office -- and if that isn't already enough, by the time I get there, there's Jessie already ensconced in their room and nailing my mike and she's going nonstop like she was made for it, you betcha, going:

> *(In the new room setting, JESSIE simply takes his mike, slides centre focus, and:)*

JESSIE: *What can I say to the panting public? Choof-choof, always on the choof-choof, isn't she ever. They nicked her trying to run a red light. Dangerous driving in charge of a wheelchair; what sort of rhubarb is that? You're off the road for keeps, the beak orders her. Oh yeah? Eat this one; it squeaks, she says and gives the beak the right royal digit. She just trades up for a Wheelchairs-R-Us Shag-Magnet 4WD mean machine with ochre-n-black trim and matching muddies and Blackpowers-R-Us pennant flag with tungsten frame, bull-bars rhino-strength and hunting lights to freeze a charging buffalo or any bank you know back. Gears? They'd grind away your back teeth and they're driving Bridgestone 275s on Dirty Dog wheel trims, enough to make Everest look an anthill. Anyway, there I am tossed out of another kitchen waiting for any lift I can get on the first road I can make it to and suddenly there's Tru gunning smoke outa twin spoilers as she pulls over on the track out of Hobart. 'Hop on', she says. 'No worries', I says. Halfway across Bass Strait I finally get to yell out at the top of this dirty big brute of a breaking wave we're shaggin' zooming over, 'How come the mainland?' And my Tru, she's yelling back, the silly old moll: 'I might be the pick o' them all, but the only piece of me Tassie's getting is the back of my big black bum!'*

(She flippantly tosses the mike back to GEORGE AUGUSTUS R., and disappears from view.

While GEORGE AUGUSTUS R. speaks, lighting up on GEORGE AUGUSTUS R.'s aspects of TRU and JESSIE's room as he describes them:)

GEORGE AUGUSTUS R.: So, I've beetled down the corridor behind them when around the corridor suddenly I'm getting introduced to their twin-share suite like the old-boner near-goner brochure says, like as if your imagination's seeing rainbow instead of dog squirt. There's chaos there that'd shame my room and I live in that out of real disgust. Like, over the TV there's humungous red satin bloomers Queen Victoria would've played rugby in and they're out drying off the try line or something. There's bottles and jars and sticky crunched-up kleenexes that I still don't want to think about. I'm there getting into asthma distress with a fog of talcs and, you-don't-have-to-be-Einstein, false-teeth glues, probably doubling up fixing wigs on too. But at least, see, outside that French door caper there's a real cheery little garden all tizzied up with flowers and what gardens have. Trouble is this French door isn't open to letting fresh air in; and also there's like this something-else smell not quite right, like. I'm thinking zoos and I'm like thinking lion cages and that blood'n'bone finger-down-the-throat smells you get in zoos, right? And I'm watching both of them pulling back the curtain that's around one of the beds like it's Chinese royalty inside and holding out this like long-dead ham sandwich they've pinched from the lunchtime sitting I guess and Tru's going... get this:

9

The Lizard of Oz
TRU: Ooo's my pretty boy then?

GEORGE AUGUSTUS R.: …and Jessie's going:

JESSIE: Ooo's our own King Billyboy, give's a smack on the lippy-lips.

> *(When the bed mosquito curtain is pulled back,*
> *there stands, so immobile as possibly set in stone*
> *and outfitted as GEORGE AUGUSTUS R.*
> *describes, BILLYBOY)*

GEORGE AUGUSTUS R.: And there's me suddenly looking at this goanna thingo, big mothafrrrukker, dinosaur nightmare come true, over there on the pillow there like it's the Lion King up on the outcrop posing for publicity stills. But it's wearing this like dog's harness on, all tartan, and there's these red bows around its revolting neck and revolting tail and all these Smiley stickers stuck along its back, I mean really badly like dog-ears. And it's going dead still like its contemplating the survey of all it commands and it's got this upchuckka of a purple tongue uggers thing lolling out of the side of its upchuckka of a mouth thing. Meantime old Tru and Jessie, they're still trying to tempt it with this dry old ham sandwich going:

TRU: Oos…?

JESSIE: Oos…?

GEORGE AUGUSTUS R.: 'Oos' this and 'Oos' that…
>   *(as best possible, BILLYBOY reacts as:)*
…when all of a suddenlike like it snatches it, raises its revolting head to dragon's heaven or whatever-takes-you and swallows the bread to halfway and then stops like a

10

statute of the Lion King somebody's shoved his half-finished sarny into the mouth of in the middle of Trafalgar Square or somewhere.

(pause)

Did I say how it's got these false eyebrows the old girls've eye'liner'd in? And the pink bow around its neck, oo-la-la on the side like? See, you can't miss that?

(pause)

So there's me cooling my heels in the doorway when, like sudden, I'm guessing I must be in like Flynn, whoever that is, or something, and old Tru, she's going to me like I've just been passed into some secret society:

TRU: (proudly pointing to BILLYBOY) Scoffing his greens puts hair on his little chest.

GEORGE AUGUSTUS R.: ...and Jessie nodding seems-you're-family-now-mate and going:

JESSIE: Call him Billyboy, or your majesty King Billy will do, or up your flue.

GEORGE AUGUSTUS R.: And there's me suddenly a camera lens like, eyeball to eyeball with life-as-the-great-scaley-nightmare, like trying to get across to each other what life's being eaten and not being eaten is all about... thinking how do you work Godzilla the goanna into oral history to impress they-who-the-piper-pay back at the office?... when Jessie snatches the mike away from me again, going rat-tat nonstop you'd-better-believe-it:

(JESSIE has done so, has slid front and centre again; is full of protective aggression)

JESSIE: *Hey, hey, what can I say? We're just past Flinders Island when my Tru cops sight of old Bill Lanne*

11

hauling in this whale, bleeding all over the place, both of them. I'm sorry more for the whale in the hands of that big black blowhard m'self because they should've been boiling his blubber down for candles not the whale, but Tru's coming alongside him n' his ship batting her eyebrows and wriggling her hips and she's calling 'Ahoy you can come alongside of me anytime, you big one-left hunk, you'. 'Hop on Bill!', she shouts into the Roaring Forties funnily off Antarctica. 'No way Ugly', the so-called last of the Tasmanian males, useless as my fanny all of 'em, burps back to my Try. But Tru, she was a goner for him right from the start, couldn't you tell, right? So we end up choof-choofing around that Bass Strait in the wake of that rotgut of a whaler like a lovesick seagull, her not me. Tru's gunned the Shag Magnet down to twenty-five fathoms to rescue his false teeth. She's thundered alongside when he threw his breakfast up over the side and she's bottled it in case he needed its vitamins later, never mind poor Shag Magnet's duco. She's followed him ashore to shaggin' Hobart Town, George Town, Queenstown, all the whitie shaggin' towns before Van Diemen's Land got stuck with Tasmania -- or that's what they told me anyway and what do I know? Old Bill couldn't stagger out of a Ladies' Lounge without my Tru waiting there outside for him and then she's parading the Shag Magnet before him wherever he staggers and falls dead drunk onto the running board and my Try's only always nudging me over going 'Make way for King Bill, the only man in the world for a gal', and showing the black-rights flag in the form of a crayon drawing before it seen a needle'n'thread, and her trumpeting 'MAKE WAY FOR HIM WHO'S NOW ME ONE'N'ONLY, NO BULL ALL BILL! MAN MOUNTAIN COMING THROUGH!' to all and shaggin' sundry, never mind embarrassing yours truly as white-as-snow as they come, ain't I ever. The pubs closed, there bloody Bill'd be flaked over the Shag

Magnet's handlebars like Lord Muck of the Fowlhouse as though that Sailor's Rest was a palace not a doss-down. I mean. Only that time when the real lah-de-dah Prince of Wales bowls up to meet him aboard the real royal yacht do we hang back on the tide. Yeah, my Tru's hanging back on the tide for the first time in her life! And by this time all the smarmies're calling him King Billy too on account he's near enough to being the last of the Tassie mob, as close as Bill Lanne would ever get to this side of the law, let me shaggin' tell you, and after that all we're doing is dodging paparazzi whatcumcallits and other socialite scumbags while we're propping him up on the floorboards drunk as a skunk and twice as salty as he drunkenly goes dispensing holey dollars like it's confetti they've given him as dolled-out charity like, but he's too silly in the beanbag to know it. I'm telling you all this cos there was nothing my Tru wouldn't do for that man. We rode the whale's back so he wouldn't have to strain his harpoon eye. We towed their carcasses back to the big boat so poor little Billy-willy wouldn't get splinters rowing too hard or callouses on his widdle hands. Even in the teeth of the Southerly, you could hear them all sniggering, bloody old Bill's got his hooks into a bit of a boongy bint; fate worse than death with a wilted wonker. And if you listened right you could hear my Tru crying out inside, 'He's me last man, ever, no bull!' That's the hard bit, see. And me trying to point out, 'He is the last, Tru, no bull'. And she screaming back, not like her, 'What's the diff, dopey? What's the time lag?' Me, I never could say; what time lag? What do I know? She was never the same much again...

(She flips the mike back to GEORGE AUGUSTUS R. and returns to TRU and BILLYBOY, relit)

13

The Lizard of Oz

GEORGE AUGUSTUS R.: And that's just half of it. I mean, doesn't the word come from the office they want Billyboy on tape before he fluffs it. 'Get the King', they say. So I'm trying. I'm doing my best here out in the field alone like. And I still reckon you can hear Billyboy give this big burp right now and again, turn the amp up like. And I'm saying to m'self: forget oral histories like, what I could be recording is a first recorded history of some dinosaurus-type reptilean monstrosity going burp-wise on tape, and on cue. I mean, back at the office they-who-the-piper-pay've told me how Billyboy's been with the old girls for five years or more, no bulling around, and like how they'd kept him hidden in the closet of that near-goner's doss-out, don't ask me how. Even there, you'd twig the staff must've thought old Tru and Jessie were a bit more on the nose than a couple of old ducks have a right to be, right?

TRU: (tickling it) Oos our pretty boy?

JESSIE: (ditto) Oos our 'andsome Billy-lilly?

GEORGE AUGUSTUS R.: Anyway first recording of a dirty great goanna belch or not, on cue or not like, when Billyboy does it, they're suddenly two sweet old ladies, sitting all prim like, hands in laps, ankles together, lips going that zipped-up thing. And I'm suddenly thinking would butter melt in their mouths or was it already dribbling out the sides? And they're waiting for me to ask what them-who-the-piper-pay say I've got to ask, so I ask:

(He addresses the two old ladies directly)

GEORGE AUGUSTUS R.: Say, ladies, what would you say to Life Itself if it were standing before you right now?

14

TRU: I'd say suck on this; it might've been in a jam

JESSIE: Me, I'd go for its crutch with me knee, kapow!

TRU: I'd say sit on this before I sit on yours.

JESSIE: Hey, Life droopy-drawers or whatever y'shaggin' name is, get back in line with all the other lover boys.

GEORGE AUGUSTUS R.: And then I go the usual number-two follow-up:
(addresses them directly again)
Like, when did you pop out?

TRU: Y'joking? One stroke of me little fanny and I never stopped popping out.

JESSIE: Don't ask me, I never stopped popping either, although mine were more like close-the-doors-n-pull-down-the-blinds.

GEORGE AUGUSTUS R.: No, I think they mean when you were born.

TRU: Born? Well before I started popping out, I can tellya.

JESSIE: Born? I was born before they had any borns. If you weren't quick, you'd end out in the mud with the 'tatta peelings.

TRU: (brushing her off) I got born in 1803 before anyone bothered with borns or 'tatta peelings.

GEORGE AUGUSTUS R.: (disbelief) '1803?'

TRU: (high horse) Who said 1803?

JESSIE: You did.

TRU: I said thereabouts, dopey.

JESSIE: (turning on him) See? Wax outa the shell-likes, sonnyjim.

TRU: (sweetly) See, I was born in a rock pool, in a water pond, in the lilies of a dancing tide out Derwent way, and real lovely it was. Made you open your nostrils and want to pop out.

JESSIE: I got spat out down a tin mine in Dorset n' never had a strong chest.

TRU: (put down) Not a tit in sight.

JESSIE: Hey!

TRU: Hey y'dopey self!

JESSIE: Hey!

TRU: Hey!

> *(GEORGE AUGUSTUS R. has to turn away from them)*

GEORGE AUGUSTUS R: All right, back at the office they're not too happy with the answers, so tell me something new. Anyway, how does that help me there, stuck in the getting-it-all-down's time warp, somehow

finding myself in a world where I'm gawking away at that wheelchair of hers... I'm talking old Tru here... and thinking she's in this near-goners' joint and she's still sitting in it like it's some, yeah, throne and I'm going sorry-sorry-I-asked and keeping my mouth clammed after that. Back at the office they-who-the-piper-pay are riding me why I gave up at that point, switch the recorder off; it's oral history; it's belongs to us more than just hers – and all that stuff, nor yours to wonder why, kid. Hey, who's a kid? Well, it might be like oral history to them but it's all rubbery to me. I rubber, you wobble, right? I mean, didn't I try to get onto that old Jessie too:
(he turns directly to her)
Jessie?

JESSIE: You'd be lucky, sport.

GEORGE AUGUSTUS R.: Sorry?

JESSIE: Nobody throws their leg over me.

TRU: Me neither.

JESSIE: Not until I make m'self a bit lady like, they don't.

TRU: Ain't it true!
(to him)
Start pumping a bit more iron, honeypie.

GEORGE AUGUSTUS R.: (next question) And when did you get a look in, Jessie?

JESSIE: You cheeky b.
(but snatches the mike from him and launches herself front and centre again for a quick:)
17

The Lizard of Oz

Don't ask me where, what do I know?, 'cepting it was close to where the migrant ship left from in Pommyland and when it finally got to dock at that Melbourne wharf there, where didn't I ever stand on that gangplank because nobody's going to throw their leg over me, and I yelled down to all those horny Eye-tites down there on the dockside looking for a bit even if they had to take a bride to get it, and I gave them a real cop of an eyeful and then gave it to them straight, 'Righto, who's game?'.

TRU: Nobody would've been.

JESSIE: Hey!

TRU: They weren't all silly in the head in those days!

JESSIE: Hey!

TRU: Hey, root yer boot!

JESSIE: Hey, root your boot!

GEORGE AUGUSTUS R.: (simply turning away) This Jessie, she's so skinny, it's like when she clacks those dentures, it's like her bones are breaking. Old Tru's as black as the ace of spade but all shiny like you'd like to dive into her when the full moon's going and you can see the moonlight go splat-splat. So this is what they're saying oral history for real, I'm going to myself, and, well, you can blow her down, and in the silence that follows that doesn't stop old Jessie nailing my mike again going here-we-go-the-ridgy-didge again:

> *(JESSIE has done exactly that, now front and centre again)*

18

JESSIE: *What can I say you ain't heard? My Tru bawled her eyes out after they found old Bill, big celebrity by then, in the lane and then laid him out, then sliced his head open to pinch his skull not an hour onto that-there death bed. Then after the rotten government mob sawed off his poor old hands and feet just so's no thievin'- magpie crowd would have his whole skeleton to hawk around, she bawled her eyes out. That's my Tru I'm talking about. Then after that, that shaggin' night, after they dug up n' robbed what was left of old Bill that'd been put in a grave, my Tru, she bawled her little eyes out. What could I do? King Billy gone, then gone into pieces. 'Tell me, lovie', I go to her, 'which piece did you love the best and we're going after that, too right', but now they started calling her Queenie, would you believe. Queen Tru, and I'm spending all my time on Shag Magnet's buckboard trying to sink the boot in keeping them off from all coming at her with calipers trying to measure her konk and which piece of her's going to fit in their jars. 'You shags wanna know what size she is?', I'm going, sinking the boot in right, left n' centre, 'I'll tell you shags: She wears one-size-fits-all New-York-Yankee's baseball cap', I yell out but you don't hear anyone laugh? No, now they're all dead serious to get at her and she's my Tru! And, listen, yous, meantimes they've got chocks under the Shag Magnet's Bridgestones and sinking their claws in real strong. The Shag Magnet's roaring to get on, but they're pumping her with all these questions with pens n' notepads n' press passes stuck in their greasy hats and there's whole horizons of them, I kid you now, in white coats n' government ties'n'collars too. Then one day my Tru grabs me and crushes herself into me and I cradle her and my Tru cries out, 'Don't let them cut me up!', she screeches. 'Don't let them cut me up too!', she cries. No way little lady, I go; no way, my Tru; we're getting out of here! And I shove her into the passenger seat and I took*

19

The Lizard of Oz
the wheel m'self and I gunned old Shag Magnet down the
Derwent and we sailed off high into the sunset and at 110
kilometres I levelled her out and tell her it's all right now
Tru my Tru, and we put our heads down and we sleep the
sleep of the innocent at Zero G for, what?, maybe 10 or
20 or so Ashes series, until one day she moved my over
and shooed off the family of wedgetails and put the old
foot down, right hand down back down to little planet in
the big wide universe they call Earth again. 'Let 'em
come!', she shouted. 'Do your worse!', she shouted. This
is my Tru. 'Up all of youse', she shouted. And we
whooped and we waved and we went a bit ratbaggery!
We caught this real beauty of a boomer and surfed its
dump and we slid all the way down its great face and we
freestyled right across the beach there at Warrnambool,
down Timor Street past the Civic Centre, up north to the
Murray, through the orchards in citrus, like, and onto the
Dig tree and a turn or two around Burkie and Willsie's
ghosts, hammered along with a wurly-wurly northeast-
like to nail the Opera House with a few hoony wheelies,
crashed the Dividing Range like piss-all until we laid
down rubber along a few of those Barrier reefs off
Cairns, no sweat n' bugger the greenies, burned off the
crocs at Kakadu, showed them a thing or two, bombed out
Broome like they thought the Japs were back with a
vengeance to pick up their empty shells, then touched
down light as a flibberty feather, three-point job, neat and
nice, tidy as you like, on the top of Ayers Rock at sunset.
Lovely, it was. Purple dye, it was. 'Uluru', Truggie
sighed. Oo-roo to you too, I sighed all giggly. Safe at
last. Spot on at last. Ozzies. Basked in deep'n'dark
ruby. I tell you.

(After pause, she flips mike back to GEORGE
AUGUSTUS R., and returns to her TRU, now

20

*strangely picking up BILLYBOY and retreating
slowly from the light into a corner)*

GEORGE AUGUSTUS R.: (pointing out TRU's
movements) Don't ask me what she is doing, not then or
now, ask me like. See how slow old Tru is moving now
view-wise? Old Jessie too. The two of them, likeasif
they're in the land of Billyboy and
watching'n'waiting'n'not moving a muscle is the zippiest
thing going around town. This, is what I was trying to tell
them-who-the-piper-pays back at the office. You hit the
Slo-Mo. Don't ask me why. It's the go, no-go is. Click,
it's on. Click, it's off. Suddenly you look down and click,
it's on again and you see the timer's gone way on. Like,
you see you've been, you-know, initiated into the tribe is
for the whole last week and when you roll it we see how
I've gotten myself into being Billyboy's babysitter while
them two lovely ladies, creak-creak, squelch-squelch, take
off as soon as I front up each day, going giggling down
the corridor and coming back only when visiting time's-
up, smelling of like chocolate and gin. Okay, if it's not
gin, it ain't no roses, either. And then someone's hit the
fast forward and there I am arriving just when the near-
goners' place's Manager bad-arse's foghorner voice,
y'know?, is coming all down upon old Tru there, in her
room, on her old knees, wailing… and you just know like
you're walking in on something terrible you don't get in
your normal oral histories.

(This scene comes to light behind him.

*The MANAGER's actual presence or silhouetted
presence is looming.*

*TRU is on her knees with old Jessie's trying to hoist
her up into the wheelchair but not succeeding. TRU*

> *is holding BILLYBOY in her hands. It is not moving*
> *but lies sideways across her palms. Its tongue is*
> *lolling to one side. Its red tail ribbon is like*
> *dangling. All the Smiley stickers have fallen off on*
> *the floor. Its eyeliner is all smudged. It is lifeless.*
>
> *JESSIE is endeavouring to help TRU lift BILLYBOY*
> *into her lap without easy success. This is difficult*
> *because she too is in grief, cradling its cheek*
> *against her own, and trying to blow into its nostril*
> *at the same time.)*

GEORGE AUGUSTUS R.: What can I tell you more than what's unwinding before you? 'Cept for old Tru's heart-wrenching sobbing away's like, you know? I'm stopped. I'm stoppered, like. Suddenly there's soundproofing all over the world. 'Cepting too for old Jessie's huffing'n'puffing into Billyboy's real gross nostrils, spew, like she's practicing the tuba or something. I'm thinking a fit coming. But old Jessie's holding both of them sort of from falling over going:

JESSIE: Ssh ssh. Ssh ssh. Ssh ssh.

TRU: (terrible outcry) Don't let them cut me up!

JESSIE: No way, no way!

GEORGE AUGUSTUS R.: (shocked himself) And then there's that Manager of the dump and he's there unmoved, like his shoulder blades are glued together, and he's going, teeth shut n' lips all mealy-mouthed:

MANAGER: Who did this will get it, but we don't have lizards in this establishment. If we do lizards have to be

unmoving, and if unmoving they definitely are required to
be alive. It's as simple as that.

GEORGE AUGUSTUS R.: And I'm with Tru and Jessie
in giving him the big I for ignore and they-who-the-piper-
pay back at the office are asking me what's happening. I
go I tell you what's happening: Tru's lifting Billyboy up
to me... like why to me?... and her big near-goner eyes
are great crying pools like you have to be there to
properly see, and my own chest's going real tight and
then, would you believe?, she's only crawling out through
those French door things to the garden outside...
　　　(as TRU does so)
yes, on her knees, you blind?... yes, yes... outside to their
garden thingo out there, yes, right? I mean, is she going
to make it? And Jessie she's with Tru and on her knees
too. And they're both suddenly on all fours clawing at the
ground out there with their bare hands... nutty-mad like,
digging a grave for Billyboy with their own bare hands.
Jesus H.

MANAGER: (from inside) No grave digging sans
permission, oh no.

　　　*(He gets no response, swings around to GEORGE
　　　AUGUSTUS R.)*

MANAGER: Nobody's allowed to say we allow that
around here!

GEORGE AUGUSTUS R.: ('don't look at me') I'm told
to say it's oral history, dude.

MANAGER: Nobody's allowed to tell you that around
here!

The Lizard of Oz
GEORGE AUGUSTUS R.: How's about I tell you
'Sayonara', then?
    (and)
So I'm about to take off back to the office to tell them-
what-the-piper-pays I don't dig this oral history caper all
of a sudden, like, when old Jessie's up and she's at my
mike again, like there's this genie out of the bottle and
she's gasping-crying-whispering-going like I'm thinking
she's a goner this time for sure:

> *(JESSIE takes the mike from him; she is mightily
> distressed but not as bad as he makes it sound. She
> is more white-hot angry-frustrated:)*

JESSIE: *What can I say but you should've copped a load
of the two of us up there on the Rock, on top of, oh, Oz
world and didn't all those daylets set on the daylight let!
Not an inch of the Shag-Magnet's treads moved from
there, yet we spun in the swoon of the great rock's eve-
tiding, its amethyst in-swathed. When the great dog
hooted at the drunken bo'sun moon, we lay the evening of
our lives down in it and I think I heard my Tru's dreaming
of huge snake coilings, immense gorgings of the pig rats,
hummings-along in the all-of-times, in the never-never
evers of the Ancestors, and there were moanings there
and groanings there and the gay-lauds of all the tribes of
her there as all sparks flibberted moon-wooed up and
flittered over and over and over all. The lair the moon.
The carve drawings caved. She softed and I heard. The
lair the moon such a big larry, ha ha. She if-ted and I
hah-ed. Then she vibrated and shook me and nodded and
let off the Shag-Magnet's triple-bypass, chip-on-board
hand brakes, and there we were back in present time and
don't we ever lazily roll down in rivulets to the floor of
the great rock, paddling across the soft Gibson, bird-
tracking the Diamantina-ville with the dreamed Spirit,*

creaking at Coopers and buzz the bejesus out of the termites in the black stump where my Tru, she says, 'Got here finally', and I say, 'Where?', and she just points down to our Billyboy there, proud as a peacock as any great goanna could be, and says, 'Where else, dopey?'. You can believe this or not. And all she had to do was lean out over the driver's side and there he was, proud as punch, his widdle neck already cocked for the scratchies chooy-coo and his tail going swish on the wag and swoosh on the wag, and she clucking, 'That's my widdle Billyboy; oo's my King Billy, that's oo you are'. Well, it's the first time I'm seeing and hearing her talk like to old Bill, so I say, 'What is that, Tru?, I ask and who wouldn't? But Tru, she says, 'Hey, dopey, d'you think we Tassie mob put all our eggs in one whaling basket they could dig up n' chop to pieces? He's me one'n'only and very last, no bull', she says. And from that time on... from the first and last...Tru's Billlyboy always rode the Shag Magnet on me lap. What a lovey-dovey! What a peach of a purple flickerer! See this lap too? I'm tellingya, a real man deserves nothing less than this lap here, see.

(She flips the mike back to the MANAGER, who doesn't want it, who flips it back to GEORGE AUGUSTUS R., who doesn't now want it much but has to take it. She returns to sobbingly help TRU cover BILLYBOY's grave with their bare hands.

A blackout.

When lighting returns, it is the next morning light.

GEORGE AUGUSTUS R. is trying to get past the MANAGER who is 'stuck' in the doorway of their room. He stubbornly thwarts any outsider getting in past him.

Inside the room, there's TRU collapsed out on the floor in the corner by the French door, flopped out like a rag doll with her head shaking on her chest and perhaps moaning, but smally.

JESSIE is kneeling by her side, where else?, and she's prodding a cup of tea at TRU over and over, but with deadpan and fruitless gestures, all dead weight to it, going to TRU with each prod:)

JESSIE: Tea. Tea. Tea. Tea. Tea…

(The MANAGER is loud)

MANAGER: There's her banana cake specially made.
    (no reaction from TRU or JESSIE)
She can go out onto the road and attack tyres.
    (still no reaction)
She can keep the TV control.

(JESSIE gives him a defiant raspberry.

The MANAGER whips around to GEORGE AUGUSTUS R.)

MANAGER: She can't do that to me, an impeccable livelihood with only natural deaths!

GEORGE AUGUSTUS R.: I bet.

MANAGER: Nobody goes downhill so fast, not on my watch, you don't!

(The MANAGER storms off.

GEORGE AUGUSTUS R. looks into the room, sees the scene. He sees too that outside in the garden, the grave they have dug for BILLYBOY has been grossly and crudely disturbed.

He hesitates only for long enough for JESSIE to look up and see him and to point terribly out to the violated grave before finding it too much to contemplate coping with.

He turns and hurries off too, after the MANAGER.

JESSIE returns to pushing the cup at TRU.

Blackout.

Long pause in silence before slow spot comes back on GEORGE AUGUSTUS R.:)

GEORGE AUGUSTUS R.: I know what you're thinking. Hey, I'm just what they send and then switch on and switch off, yeah? I said it. I said okay I'm just the Recorder. But they still sent me back. I said, bugger this; you know what you can do with your oral history. But, see, they still sent me back. I said I can't. They said yes you can. You are part of us and we are the piper paid and paying. But you don't know what there, I said. Yes, we do, they said; it's always happening; it just needs the recording, son.
        (his voice goes low recounting:)
I'll tell you what maybe you couldn't see too clearly…
        (and)
See, the thing is, someone had dug Billyboy back up from where they had buried him with their old own near-goner hands. Someone had chopped off his tail and left it there by the grave they'd dug with their own bare mitts.

27

The Lizard of Oz

Someone had chopped off his head and left it there by the grave deliberate like, like use this as soup stock you old farts. Someone had lopped off his revolting little legs and left them there by the grave. Someone had left his tartan harness and his red bows lying there. Someone had stuck a couple of those Smiley stickers on the French doors by the grave. No one had left his little torso there. That was gone. Was the main part of Billyboy's body. See, this like trail of blood wound off from his little grave there and disappeared into the grass around the place, and all it's supposed to be is a near-goner place. I'm looking at it and I'm thinking like sinkhole, vanished. And I'm saying this but I still don't think it's right.

> *(Lighting back on TRU and JESSIE.*
>
> *It is obviously the next evening. TRU is now encased in a wheelchair. She remains lifeless, unresponding.*
>
> *Still kneeling besides her (of course!), JESSIE keeps forlornly adjusting the blanket around her and gently pushing the cup of tea to her lips. Weeps escape from her.*
>
> *The MANAGER has come back with GEORGE AUGUSTUS R. and his tone tartily expresses it is the end game:)*

MANAGER: (more at the other man) We have walking tours and the shopping buses here. We have music hour. We have Snakes & Ladders and the daily rags. Nobody goes downhill without reason here, but you get to the stage you just want to throw up your hands.

GEORGE AUGUSTUS R.: (appalled at what he is seeing) I bet.

MANAGER: (pompous) Don't get into the business of trying to help.

GEORGE AUGUSTUS R.: You bet I won't.

(The MANAGER storms out.

GEORGE AUGUSTUS R. is left alone with TRU and JESSIE.)

GEORGE AUGUSTUS R.: (sotto voce) Someone had left no flowers in their little garden.

JESSIE: Tea. Tea...

(As if she asked for it, he steps forward and offers the mike to JESSIE.

She takes it but doesn't raise from her knees, and:)

JESSIE: *Where was I? Star lines shucked us and we took little Billyboy up pointed at the horizon. 'Where to now?', I shouted into the slipstream 'Into the lovely wind in my hair', my Tru was laughing at last and I heard fly by little Billyboy'n'me the way she said: 'We're going where we are safe where the ham sandwiches are the real hot-diggery'. See?; oh, did you see with us?, how the rainbow serpent, I saw as I've seen, chuckled and swaged in the steeps of the flooding inland sea as we floated by on a carpet a-flowering in neutral. Bloom and blush hush-a-bye Australia's land can. 'Take tea', I said. 'Don't let them cut me up too, but bury me behind the mountains', she said, did my Tru. 'Drink some tea', I said. It's only*

*tea. It's free. It'll do you good. Don't let them cut me up,
promise again, but bury me behind the mountains, oh.
Take tea, I tell her. Tru, drink tea now; it seeps down
through the ages-oh. Tru. My Tru. Queenie. My Queen
Tru that you are.*

    (She stops, holding the mike out in space, in limbo.

    He gently takes it from her)

GEORGE AUGUSTUS R.: It's near the end of what I
can come away with. Is that the world fullstop?, I ask
they-who-the-piper-pay. It happens all the time, they-
who-piper-pay said. Bash that, I said. Bashing that
happens all the time too, they said. It's just extinction
being forever, give or take a day. Well, I tell them, you
can fug off with your extinction, like. What's extinction
when it's home when it always turns up like a bad penny
the next day?
    (gets familiar with audience)
You know it's sinkhole of a wheelchair, right?
    (and)
You come to realise that when there's no change day after
day. Soon, the end of days. Old Tru. Queen Tru. Queen
Tru. I'm seeing her as a pile of ash against the light of
that day. But they're still sending me and Jessie, she's
kneeling down beside her Tru, waving us all off and like
I'm guessing it's the same cup of tea like they-who-piper-
pay say it always is and she, Jessie, she's prodding away
still, going:

JESSIE: Don't cry. Tea. Take tea…

    *(But she does look up and she maybe fully sees
    GEORGE AUGUSTUS R. for the first real time and*

*she gets up and takes the mike hardily from him
again.*

*She is as forthright as before, front and centre, and
it is almost as though you will have to slow it down
to hear her right:)*

JESSIE: What can I say when I know she is leaving? I
kept saying to my Tru, 'Don't cry'. And she keeps saying,
'Who's crying, dopey?'. And I keep saying, 'Tru, don't
cry'. And my Tru, she keeps saying, 'Who's crying?'
'Don't cry', I said. 'Who's crying?', she kept up. 'Don't
go crying', I'm saying, oh. 'Who's going crying?', she
said. Don't cry. Tru. Don't cry...

(end)

The Lizard of Oz

Blind Freddie's Laments

(a groping monologue)

Blind Freddie's Laments

With life currently blindsiding him just as genetics always has, unsighted Henry indulges himself in the guilty pleasure of self-misery in the form of Blind-Freddie lamentations to his two leading tormentors – his wife Clarissa and God. In that order. But these are nothing to what cannot be stopped nor stoppered in his lamentations upon his lost daughter.

With the loss of his last eye some months ago, the world he knows now is only his chair and its side table, his telephone and his radio and their metaphorical cords tailing off beyond arms-reach. Where these lead he can never see again, and the silences that come to him these last days pulse to overwhelming.

Cast

HENRY GASSER   (very much alone)

Setting

One man alone on stage, with perhaps a chair and a small side table. To reflect his lack of visibility, it is recommended that the stage be darkened and he spotlit.

Blind Freddie's Laments

*(On the stage, only HENRY GASSER isn't
blackened completely out.*

*The world he knows now is only his chair and its
side table, his telephone and his radio and their
metaphorical cords tailing off beyond arms-reach.
Where these lead he can never see again, and the
silences that come to him these last days pulse to
overwhelming.*

*Only the voices in the hot twilight, in his dimming
of dreams, in his eyes out of the blank, in his phone
off and on the speaker...)*

1. Blind Freddie talking to a wife

HENRY: Hey!
  (nothing, so he calls)
CLARISSA? MY PEE AND YOUR LEG, CLARISSA!
  (waits)
Clarissa? Look, Jesus H.!, don't go yet.

CLARISSA'S VOICE: No?

HENRY: You're a stubborn woman, Clarissa. I know
you're thinking there he is trying to be all fanny uptight
again. I do not think you climaxing throughout the whole
house is funny in any fanny way. You try laughing at your
witching-hour caterwauls, Clarissa. You've always
confused passion with breaking wind. Am I so pathetic?

Blind Freddie's Laments

If you think acting out Vladimir Nabokov's Laughter in the Dark is funny, who's pathetic? Duh, you're the wife and that bugger you've got there is the lover, and you're having a real giggle slurping just out of blind-man's-bluff-reach of poor old blind cuckold blind-freddie hubby me. Jesus H., Clarissa, get an imagination.

(sudden shout)

CLARISSA?, YOU THINK YOU'VE GOT TITS, BUT THEY'RE PAINT JOBS!

(calms)

You say you're really taking off this time but that could just mean you're growing mould, bloody Clarissa. I don't deserve that... slurping noise. Look, if you're going, take my father's books, stuff n' things. Shit, don't keep saying you don't want them; it's his fortieth again soon. You know there'll be yet another bloody medal for his memory called the Cranium Calipers or fart-what and, if I don't get rid of them, how can I claim I wouldn't lower myself to give to the bloody nation anything he left me to give to the bloody nation? Bugger the nation; did the bloody nation offer a crowbar or something to uncrate any of it? Crowbars enter a man's life, Clarissa, and a man's on the hook for the rest of his days.

(then whine)

But leave his pickle jars. Promise me you won't take his pickle jars, Clarissa!

CLARISSA'S VOICE: Shall I leave the door a-jar?

HENRY: Ho ho, Clarissa. What's that perfume, anyway? Verde de gris. Some whale's gut spill. Nice-to-be-alive day outside, is it, or just trying to hide your athlete's foot? And don't think I can't smell testosterone when it's passing through, bloody Clarissa. You tell the bloody man he's too near! You know I'm not a brave man, Clarissa!

38

CLARISSA'S VOICE: Henry, you'd hear footsteps if you were drowning.

HENRY: That all the bloody man's got, Clarissa? Clarissa's dead right there, old sausage. Yes, I'm speaking to you, you bloody man, whoever you are. No, wherever you are... so take that as a verbal coup de grace, old juice! You can go pop-goes-the-weasel with my wife, but I maintain the pretense that any author can remain dignified. They called me the Nabokov of the South Seas. Regrettably it was a once-only. My moniker was exam-set once, too. O levels and we're not speaking of bloody Clarissa's pop-spot, either. Real O levels. Son of a very glitterati professor-bodybag-artist makes good in his own right. Okay, you bloody man, maybe just once, also. So, well, that's me; nice t'meetcha. Oo, but where's me manners what's left over from being unmanned? Perhaps you haven't been formally introduced to my wife you are screwing? She is issa-to-us-all, old sauce. Light and creamy is she. Succulent as any Eurasian should be. Oft, I call her Big Mac, more than a mouthful no matter how little you can stomach. Poor she was, but sumptuous at pretending. Straight-off, we recognised our mutual penchant for promising outrageous lies.

CLARISSA'S VOICE: Then you went blind.

HENRY: Oh, ha ha, Clarissa. Very spicy. See, old cock, how my wife aims for brutal honesty too, but not above the belt. So now it's your turn for having to keep your guts protected from her garters, old sausage.
Careful what you wash for, ha ha. It's only fair. Step outside the script, bloody Clarissa.

CLARISSA'S VOICE: Oh, I'm stepping outside alright, Henry.

HENRY: CLARISSA!

CLARISSA'S VOICE: What?'

HENRY: Clarissa, don't go; I'll miss your bald bits.

CLARISSA'S VOICE: That's feeble, that is.

HENRY: (desperation) Clarissa, promise you won't leave me alone with my thoughts!

CLARISSA'S VOICE: I'm done with promising you anything anymore, Henry.

(He gathers himself)

HENRY: Look, okay, my mind might be so surge incontinent, I can't stop hearing you, bloody Clarissa, and then wanting to run for the dunny, but then, I gave you no Taj Mahal, did I? But you, you see, you never were one to realise there could only be one real Queen Mumtaz and you were way too slack, even giving her fourteen kids start. And, I know, I know, poor me, eyeless now, I never looked at you, did I? I should regret that now, though not really. How many of our six dog years would you allow as good, Clarissa?

CLARISSA'S VOICE: Five.

HENRY: There you go, then. What's wrong with that?

CLARISSA'S VOICE: Months.

HENRY: No, no, no, bloody Clarissa. My Dads used to drain his corpses into gutters alongside the dissecting table while all the cockroaches had to wait outside by the open drain. Outside. You send your cockroachy bloody man you've got there outside my house, Clarissa.

CLARISSA'S VOICE: Don't you go upsetting him.

HENRY: Jesus H., Clarissa. I'm only ancient old fart starring in some dodgy real-time remake of that Nabokov film as Dirk Bogarde as the blind old guy. Just keep the bloody man away from the pickle jars! There's half of the Pitjantjarajara tribe in those bottles. The famous half. They used to keep screaming at famous Pops to return them for burial, but he says they're snugger with him. Why not me, then, did someone ask? Why thank you. I do not return them either. They're family. They're science, bloody Clarissa. And if you're worried about your money, don't. It's too late.

CLARISSA'S VOICE: (shrewdly) What money?

HENRY: You cheated me, Clarissa.

CLARISSA'S VOICE: What money?

HENRY: I don't know how, but you cheated every penny, bloody Clarissa, and I've had my gumption of it. And then what do you do? You only start going I gave up my eyes just to spite taking you to Australia.

CLARISSA'S VOICE: I wouldn't put it past you.

(There is a car horn going obviously outside)

HENRY: What's that tooting? What's that honking?

41

CLARISSA'S VOICE: The taxi, thank God.

HENRY: (back to whine) Don't leave me alone with myself, Clarry! I'm an old man! Jesus H., I've spent my whole life trying to get someone else lumbered with me! Be fair, Clarissa!

CLARISSA'S VOICE: See you in the formaldehyde, Henry.

HENRY: All right, so go, bloody Clarissa! Flit off, you and your bloody man of a fink flitter. You think I'm going to miss you? Trying to engage your mind was like free-falling over Disneyland. Your body no longer by my side? Shee, I would've needed a penile engorgement science wasn't capable of. You slack? What's limp like melting plastic, Clarissa? You forget my father left me with body parts here that I was getting stuck with before you were born. I got aboriginal 200-year-old bits'n'pieces with makeovers that'd make your mirror want to defect. And another thing, Clarissa. You weigh any DVD you like, and then write even a thousandth of what I wrote on it, and weigh it again, and what have you got? I'll tell you what you've got, bloody Clarissa. You've got the biggest weight difference in the world, that's all. It's called literature, Clarissa. It's uplifting. It's not your sag, Clarissa. Jesus H., in a few years your crutch will be dragging lower than Skippy-the-Kangaroo's grandmother's.
    (and)
CLARISSA, I'VE BOTTOMED OUT, BUT YOUR LARDY LUMPS BEAT ME BY A MILE!

(There is silence to this, though)

HENRY: You there, Clarissa…?

(He gets nothing)

HENRY: Who's there?

(but still nothing)

HENRY: (finally, fearfully) Don't hurt me, okay? Do anything with the mind but leave the body alone, 'kay? 'Kay? Who's...?
   (can get defiant through bluster)
CLARISSA, YOU STOP THAT PANTING. IT'S LIKE HAVING TO LISTEN TO A CRACK IN THE GUTTER.

(Blackout)

2. Blind Freddie talking to The Other

   (HENRY back to being urbane. He is still addressing himself to what's around him but, this time, above:)

HENRY: I'll be honest, old custard… apart from Nabokov of the South Seas, they sometimes used to call me Gutsache. But it wasn't often as you'd like me to think. What I've been thinking is: for how long would I have to hold my breath before I hear you breathing? Past my lively time of death, ha ha? Oh yes, you'd like me to admit you're an improvement on Clarissa, I dare say, what with her inner thigh needing pest control. Of course, you're an improvement. So what do we do now we're

43

stuck with each other? Do I get some divine sign now?
I'll wait. No rush…
   (pretentious wait)
No?
   (waits for divine response again)
Blind Man's Bluff your thing? Spin me around and hoick
and honk me, is it? All I ask is you tell me if they get too
near! Sorry, sorry. Don't mind me; somebody once said
I'd hear footsteps if I was drowning. Oh, that you?
Everybody wants to get in on the act! So, old sauce, it's
you'n'me in the swim, is it? Don't mind the questions.
I'm far too dumb to ask anything awkward. One thing,
though… why the big phfutt of phfutts, old custard, when
Clarissa and I, we were going along pretty good there?
Put it this way: why did old Henry-me suddenly find he
couldn't lift blocks of concrete on the strength of the
squinty eye of his penis anymore? At least, not without
string. It was the bathos not the pathos of the thing, you
see, old pie-and-peas. Are you going to say you reached
down and touched me? Could you do me a favour and
not touch me again? Another thing I'm asking here, old
fried egg, is had you always written in I should go blind?
Where you there in Sri Lanka with Clarissa's fellow-local
surgeon chum when I said to him what're you done to my
eye, you prick? And he replied, 'Go back to Australia,
sir; you're not long-suffering enough to live here
anymore'. Cheeky bugger shoots me down with logic after
giving my eye the barbeque fork. Were you there? I
mean, shrapnel with the first, and then a fucking unknown
surgeon's rapier-wit with the second? It was the most
cerulean sapphire of the two too. Twas my light, old can-
of-worms. I canst make light of it nor, now, light work.
See how your imagery can survive dawn's light uptight?
Your poesy should purge, after all. Many pieces
immortalized upon the toilet roll and before applied to
bot. Vladimir Nabokov was my king of spending a penny

over a rhyming couplet or two. A good farter loudspeaks
literary talent. But you know all this. So, shall I
endeavour to wax lyrical too?:
  'I looked upon seeing the light-gravure/
  the altar candles were lights-out but the/
  callow lit the lit-erature.'
Perhaps needs a touch working on by someone cheeky
enough to try. But then, that's my point: as a poet, I'd
rather you just look upon me as a really dirty old man.
Call me Tiresias or call me a horse's arse. Neigh, neigh.
The thing is, as you keep showing, one cannot check
anything in before the check-out. This is blindness, and
don't think I don't appreciate your metaphor. We can
have the smarts, but life we can't see through, right? It's
very polished. But, see, you are scaring me witless here!
I want to scream my fear every minute of my waking day!
I want to screech fright at even the thought of falling
asleep! I could break down and bawl my eyes out with
such self-pity that I shock myself! This is the thing, see.
This is gone-to-shit blindness. Worse, it's added-on
bathos. The Evil Eye didn't do him. Rat fleas didn't end
it. Malaria didn't put his nuts in a vice. Not Dengue or TB
or the great naughty pretender of diseases. It wasn't even
the bloody prickly heat. Only you know, old custard, and
you're not saying.
    (pretends to 'scratch' around uninterestedly, but
    has to restart:)
Say, did I do something to you? And you were right
about Job. I haven't got one memory left that's worth the
pain either, anyway. Call me Brer Rabbit and life the tar
baby, and I'll call you right. Except, all I'm asking is why
you make us think thinking maketh the man? All thinking
ever did was invent you don't screw granny. I know
that's me being what makes Clarissa want to tear her hair
out. But, likewise, I know you and your compensating
look on the bright side. Like, cancer's just an opportunity

45

of losing weight. Right? And AIDS was nature's way of
cleaning up the world's needle industry. And every
jihadist beheading makes us better at the geography of the
Middle East. Oh, and it ain't death; it's just changing-
places while there's still room, right?

(and not being able to help it)

Look, I'm still shaking with fear here!

(gathers himself as he may)

Sorry, sorry, old cork. My poofy streak. Yellow doesn't
fade. Just wondering, though: you ever put one human
thought on the shelf of the Great Scheme of Things? Or
is it better we stick with the idea of you sort of knocking
something off the sideboard and oops, sorry, crash-tinkle
big big Bang. Sure, we get all that, but what's the big
mystery? What's the why?; or are you saying it actually
was all just a case of Misguided Elbow? Oops, how did
that get there?, is it? I mean, look at this dump. Is this a
real shithouse or what? Is that what your gift is, that I
can't see how much of a shithouse it is? You can tell me
what a shithouse it is. I won't mind. Anyway, any last
requests on, old son?

(waits)

I take that silence as a maybe. Well, I mentioned about
the dirty old man, not the poet… but I'd really like to
add… forget about my obsession with hormones and birth
canals; just don't forget how my given eyes never missed
fixing upon one of your world's wondrous dancing nates.
Not once. My missing orb's probably there staring up
skirts of a few gutter snipes from some gutter right now.
Knowing it as I do. Which I guess I never did.

(then)

Hey, Hughie, with all your great gift entailings, at least
it's a comfort knowing you have done it unto others. Do
unto others as you have done unto me.

(and)

So send her down, Hughie!

(endures theatrical pause)
Just knock two times first, okay?, so I know when to trip
daintily out of the way.

*(He seemingly ends, but there is something needling
him and he knows it. He waits as long as his sense
of being solitude can last, before:)*

HENRY: Look, I know it's being corny, but…. did you
really mean to slip me the bird when you were passing out
the dog whistles?

(Blackout)

3. Blind Freddie talking to his daughter

*(When he re-appears for this, he is first seated. He
alternates between this and standing, between being
near to the phone and not so near)*

HENRY: … Girlie, it's Dad! Is that you breathing? A
breath of you and it's bish-bash to some satellite, ha ha.
Not ridiculing; just nerves. What I wondered: did you
ever know they used to call me the Nabokov of the South
Seas? One Mister-Spot-on once said in literature I spun
the spillages. Also, I wanted to ask: has there been
another anniversary for us not speaking to each other? If
I had fingers to count them, I'd be in one of famous
Daddy's pickle jars, right? Tiny infant you with that hole
in the heart, and me born with a big hole in commitment.
See how early on we were tagged for a two-way bypass?
But I won't keep you in suspense. Here's the word
inheritance. I did; I said inheritance. I take your silence
for the sound of ears-pricking-up. Regrettably, I have

nothing, except a Centrelink card which wouldn't bring in much over there in Pommyland. The trouble is my figurative caught up with my realisable. There is, of course, all your professor-granddaddy's stuff, all his famous pickle jars of tribal bits'n'pieces. They'd still be pawnable if you find a pawn shop I never stopped looking for. You give the bits'n'pieces back and fame and fortune will await you back here in the Antipodes. But a fig for inheritance! I wanted to tell you how I loved your mother! Leaving her with a 'see-you-later-Alligator' was really off, I agree. It came out wrongly. Tell her she couldn't have lived with my sulkiness, anyway. I believe Vladimir Nabokov had the same weakness Not that you can compare your mother's stalag to his Stalin, ha ha. Incidentally, I've gone totally blind since we last had the little chat we never had. But then, what's sight but yesterday's tears, ha ha? Tell your mother, will you? She deserves a little comeback laugh on me. And tell her she came first out of three, and that, yes, I did end up in drift. Hello? Girlie? You know, just to see your face. Just to run my fingertips across your cheek. Just to see you against a dawn's slow brightening to rose. Just to have your little breath gentle against my cheek once more. Girlie! You write to me about your life! Forget thinking braille! Write to your old Dad! And I'll promise I'll kiss the cheek of my darlin' girl, and so I will!

(pause)

Hello?

(and)

Breathe, little girl. Breathe into my world. That so bad? That so not-good?

(emotionally has to start again)

Did I tell you how I donated my last eye to the developing-world's marble stocks? It was my one'n'only bluey too and it was in Sri Lanka. Well, when I say donated, I mean I said they could keepsake it if they ever

fished it out of the operating drain it'd rolled down into.
They said oops, fumble fingers. I said easy-come-easy-go
yourselves, you rotten shits. I said, when you airmail my
last good cat's-eye back to me, I might consider returning
your famous grand pop's pickle jars. Hey, I've got some
sum part to bury with dignity, too. Pickle jars? Girlie:
inheritance, thy name is pickle jars! There's eyes here
glazed cherry. There's toeses'n'noses and cancer blobs
that've fallen off tribal generations! You'll find in one a
Pitjantajara fingernail an imperial yard long and grown
after-death. They don't make formaldehyde fertilizer like
that anymore. There's a six-week-old foetus floating in
its own dream world. There's Squatter's potshot up
through Four-year-old's mouth and out the cranium, a
tollable tunnel, clean as a whistle. One you'll like is a
penis said to be King Billy's, the last of the Tasmanians.
Poor K.B., even his dick got lopped. Return all of it and
they'll give you your own name plaques beneath
exhibition cases. But not me. I'm not returning famous
daddy's stuff until they dredge out the cesspool my eye
splashed down in. You tell me how can I give them back
without showing what a shocking bloody kleptomaniac of
a grave-robbing prick your famous Grand-dads actually
was? He's family blood, you might be thinking?! He's
the old razor I'm attached to! Should I mind, all my life,
he'd just snort like a hog whenever he deigned to look at
me, and think it a great joke? I'm talking a father here.
But hey, we shared the genes of glandular secretions, and
are or aren't glandular secretions the glue of the universe?
I mated, he gave his best shot. I oozed; he oozed. I cried;
he cried. We're one secretion. He's who I'm stuck with,
and if that's the way it is, that's the way it is, even if I
never knew him from a bar of soap. So, no eye, no pickle
jars. They can all go root my boot. 'Root my boot's
Aussie for rooting my boot.
　　(seems to listen)

49

Blind Freddie's Laments
Girlie...?

> *(maybe gets a click)*

Ah, my little girl, if there was one thing out of the
millions of words I ever wrote, there's one passage that
sticks with me as being worth all the swim. It was written
for you my darling Juliet my Brenda my Caz my Sandy
my Sophie my Angela my Mary my Elizabeth my other
Sandra my Tessie my Lolly... and there has just got to be
an Ann in there somewhere. Only for you. It was my
dedication to you. Listen:

*'...oh, twill triluna trystful while the trust whimsies
true...'*

Jesus H., I can't remember it! Excusee. It's just that I get
this heavy feeling at the thought of you all. Each and
every one of you always gave me the acceleration but
kept the brakes to yourselves. When I went to say No, it
came out I Want. When I went to say I Wanted, it still
came out I Want. Look, Girlie: you tell your mother and
all of the others of her, I might have been a disaster BUT I
WAS NEVER INTELLIGENT!

> *(need to control himself)*

Sssh. Sssh.

> *(manages)*

Say, I've written down something else for you. It's
around her somewhere. But what's the point of looking; I
can't read it anyway. My silly. What's a memory of you
for anyway? The missing note said:

'When they found Blind Freddie amongst the tethers that
bind, there is not a battery which is not leaking nor a cord
not nibbled and gnawed upon. The phone in particular
was dead off the hook.'

(It is obvious he has almost finished now.

*He only has to find the emotional strain to come
out, in hushtones, with:)*

HENRY: Girlie… I just think I'm really hurting now. I think this growth behind my eye might've slipped its bonds. I just rang to tell you… when they took Caesar's knife to your mother, what a father I would have been if you had only lived.

(end)

Blind Freddie's Laments

I Don't Know What to Do with You

(short play)

Cast
RACHEL happily solitary, working alone… normally
THE MAN dares hardly to look up
various shadows or actual cast members milling around

Setting
Setting is flexible to intimate a small wayside refreshment
stop on a tourist route. The serving counter is the main
prop focus.

Synopsis
The invidious gnawing moral dilemma that imposes itself
She is a genial-enough woman whose main virtue (at least
she thinks) is minding her own business. As it is, there is
hardly enough time to get the coffee stopover joint ready
for the regular tourist bus, serve everyone in the mad-rush
time allowable before the bus driver starts hooting for
everyone to climb back on board before the schedule's
shot to pieces. But this time there is among them someone
who doesn't seem to be with anyone… someone the other
passengers definitely seem not to want to go near, not
even to help him out a bit.

There are just eyes you can't get past.

I Don't Know What to Do with You

(Rachel feels best feeling lonely. Her mother, proud from the dervish tribes of old Persia, used to say, 'You are lost only if the sun finds you out'.

Six times most days, people bustle her, but they are just tourists to the museum after all, not hot invaders her mother warned her about.

Either way, they are as the deserts, or she is. It doesn't matter. She knows the oasis of daily routine cools her from their comings-and-goings.

Already, the tourists are leaving her kiosk for the bus. She moves safely towards her routine: first, clean the coffee-machine.

This is when she becomes aware of him at the counter, his presence but a flutter.)

RACHEL: Yep?

THE MAN: Is that coffee, please?

(He is long, tall, sky-scrapper, looking down perplexed:)

RACHEL: Take-away?

55

I Don't Know What to Do with You
THE MAN: I don't want to break anything.

RACHEL: There's only paper-cups.

THE MAN: Coffee in a paper-cup, please.

> *(His hands hang by his side.)*

RACHEL: Milk?

THE MAN: What do other people do?

RACHEL: They take milk.

THE MAN: Milk, please.

RACHEL: Sugar's there.

> *(The man stares blankly way down to the bowl of sugar lumps. He is not moving.*
>
> *Rachel feels hot irritability.)*

RACHEL: They take one or two lumps.

THE MAN: One or two lumps, please.

RACHEL: You can have more.

THE MAN: Three, please.

RACHEL: Help yourself! Sorry, sorry. Working. You can sit over there.

> *(So sadly hunched into himself, the man carries his coffee like an offering and moves precisely to the*

precise bench she pointed to. This is not helping her much. He is halting her from sheltering in her routine. She has to watch him putting the sugar in the coffee with the paper-wrapping still on. He stirs it with his finger but it gets too hot.)

RACHEL: No need a finger!

THE MAN: I washed it first.

RACHEL: You're supposed to take off the paper.

THE MAN: Oh.

RACHEL: Look, it's your coffee.

THE MAN: It's good coffee.

RACHEL: You left your free biscuit.

(He blinks at her. She has to pick up, hold up, a biscuit. She feels how the shade can slide away and the sun could find you.)

THE MAN: Why did I leave it?

RACHEL: It's okay. You don't have to take a biscuit.

THE MAN: I can get the paper wrapper back real soon.

(The man is using her table and his hand to iron out the sodden sugar paper wrapping. Rachel blessedly forces herself back to cleaning the coffee-maker. But the man is standing at the counter again.)

RACHEL: What!?

I Don't Know What to Do with You

THE MAN: I enjoyed the coffee.

RACHEL: You didn't touch it.

THE MAN: It was real good.

RACHEL: Look, you on the bus?

THE MAN: We're on a day trip.

RACHEL: Who're you with?

> *(He shrugs, looks around the empty kiosk. The way he does so reminds her of how her mother scanned any horizon, squinting so hard in concentration, wary of where the sun might be.)*

RACHEL: You can wait here until the bus goes.

THE MAN: How do other people know when the bus goes?

RACHEL: Just keep your eye on the driver there.

> *(With huge relief that it's now up to the driver, Rachel can turn back to the coffee-maker again. She barely hears the driver's familiar bark.*
>
> *She hardly registers the usual horn for the usual stragglers, the crunch of the tyres on the gravel. She lets it all go, as routine must.*
>
> *As sands shift softly underfoot, the man is still seated there, alone.*

58

He has watched the bus leaving.)

RACHEL: You've missed it!

THE MAN: Is it going without me?

(Rachel scrambles in her own purse for her own mobile phone.

The bus company asks her to wait. She can't stand how the man continues to stare so dumbly at where the bus had been. She hurries outside for breeze.

The sun cruelly picks her out. Exposed to it against all her nature, she listens to the bus-company, then shouts to the man.)

RACHEL: They don't even know how you got on!

(The man stares at her with such utter dependency that she burns now with the despair she remembers in her own mother's voice.)

RACHEL: Did you stir your coffee?

THE MAN: Did I?

(Rachel reaches down to stir his coffee for him, stops, herself confused, did I do this already? She hears herself cry out:)

RACHEL: I DON'T KNOW WHAT TO DO WITH YOU!

I Don't Know What to Do with You
> *(The man covers his face with a great shame. She thinks she has fled back to the oasis of her routine, but finds she is sitting beside him.*
>
> *Silence has come as heavy as the sun of her childhood sand burns. It flares and grips their hands together.)*

(end)

I know

(short play)

I Know

It's unreasonable of her to catch him in bed with his ex-wife in the house that used to be his old marriage home and which, therefore, he still half owns. After all she was supposed to be the cheater with him on his ex-wife, not the other way around. That's just for starters when it comes to it being all her fault.

And now that she's got him started and can't stop, all the spleen that pours out before he's had his coffee is just plain deliberateness on her part. Even getting him started is because of her. It's all her fault... and talking of her faults...

The more he shouts, the more she merely mutters meekly.

How provocative of her is that?!

No wonder he storms out.

Cast

He's **A**.

> His cadence rises from defensiveness to outright fury, until he is shouting.

She's **B**.

> All sweetness and light.

Setting

The present, any time. No particular prop required.

I Know

(B. stands stoically before him, while:)

A: I haven't got a wink of shut-eye over this.

B: I know.

A: I'm not burning my bum just because of you catching me in the sack with someone who doesn't rasp sensitive skin tissue like some sandpaper I know, you-whistle-I'll-point!

B: I know.

A: She might be a slag but she used to be my wife! Who said you had a right to come barging into my family home that used to be my family home?

B: I know.

A: What was that: 'Do I turn on the flash or will it come out all right?' crap? How the hell would I know if it'd come out all right? I don't care how it comes out! It's your camera! You're standing in the doorway of my used-to-be bedroom, I'm not!

B: I know.

A: I'm not tying anything in a knot! Nuts here, lady, nuts here, not knots!

B: I know.

A: Yeah, and you think I'm as shallow as that too. Hey, who turned off the tap on a little jiggy-jiggy in the first place? Did you bother asking me 'do you mind if I turn off the tap?' Oh, no. You just turn off the tap and I get the disuse in the goolies!

B: I know.

A: Get your mind off the tap. You're obsessed with the tap. Don't think any lack of tap's automatically turns me dry too!

B: I know.

A: How can any tap turn on anyway, the way you snore?

B: I know, I know.

A: Whatareya? A man goes to the fridge and it's Kindly close the door on a fucking magnet. Up your rubber seal!

B: I know.

A: There you go again! Insinuations. Always boring in with the insinus. Everything's got to be insinu'd, niggle bloody niggle. What's this my flannel, your flannel bullshit Postit note in the bog? Jesus.

B: I know.

A: Vegemite! Is it before the United Nations' Security Council for boycotting? It's vegemite. It made my bones! It's only nation building, that's all! All I'm trying to do is have a bit of toast and veggie and you're over there making faces and going puke-puke?

B: I know.

A: It's the money! It's that purse thing from out of your
granny's bum or somewhere, picking out five cents with
your picky-picky little fingers pickitty-pick while the
whole world's waiting in line looking dagger at me like
it's my fault while the checkout sort's silently screaming
her head..,
   (draws breath)
off.

B: I know.

A: Spend something! Do a dollar without Instagramming
the World Bank! What did you donate to that Happy
Babies of Sudan or whatever it was? I tell you what you
donated. You donated my name. Jesus. Who told you I
wanted to donate anything?

B: I know.

A: How would you know? It's called talking! What's
wrong with a little 'good-morning'? What's wrong with
how's-it-hanging once in a while instead of the bottom lip
hoovering up the carpet? Stuff it! I'm an architect! They
wrote in on my degree a little morning conversation is
alright for architects. Show me where it says stay mute or
die!

B: I know.

A: Driving! Drive, shisssake! I have to be sober
watching you get pissed and rolling on the floor. Me
going to AA, suffering feeling like the Sahara Desert, but
oh no, you don't drive. You go by train? You bother

bussing? You get seen walking? Oh no, it's always got to be getting on my wheels!

B: I know.

A: You fluff! Always those squeaky little secretive things!

B: I know.

A: Fart! Here, I'll show you a proper fart!
     (tries but can't)

B: I know.

A: Nibbling. Nibble-nibble, nibble-nibble. Eat! Whack it right it into your guts! Whatareya, cwuddly wabbit?

B: I know.

A: Hey, big deal catching me and my ex in the sack! What's this standing in the doorway saying kindly don't go messing up the sheets? Whose sheets are they? I used to own those sheets. Those sheets are still half mine! But oh no, belittling. All the time you go the belittles. What's that mad moll of an ex-wife of mine supposed to think when some mad moll's standing there in the doorway saying watch out messing up
     (draws breath)
the sheets?

B: I know.

A: A big fat whopping great greasy big Mac! I'll eat it if I want. Up nibbling on your lettuce leaves!

B: I know, I know.

A: Dandruff! Shoot me for having it! Draw and quarter me. You, you think what's on you is just the ski season? And another thing…
> *(struggles to bring anything else to mind)*

and…
> *(sudden re-thought)*

Hair hanging outa your ears! Hairy lip! Jesus, who has to pluck between their toes?!

B: I know.

A: Great hairy thighs! Great hairy armpits! Somebody get onto Melbourne Zoo! Shaving your fanny? It's like trying to squeeze moisture out of a porcupine!

B: I know.

A: Pimples! Jesus, who has to go the squeeze anymore like you gotta? Ping, against the bathroom mirror! Choice!

B: I know.

A: You keep aspirin. You keep paracetamol. You keep naproxen. You keep ibuprofen. You keep Tums. You keep Lomotil.

B: I know.

A: You keep Oxazepam. You keep acetaminophen. You keep prozac. You keep dematol. You keep…

B: I know.

I Know

A: … I haven't finished! You keep… pacerone! You keep halotussin. You keep tadafil. You keep… that… zanamirlalalala thing. What am I supposed to be, a chemist?!

B: I know.

A: YOU LEAK!

B: I know.

A: (sarcastic) 'I know'?!

B: I know, I know.

A: 'I know, I know'?!

B: I know, I know, I know.

A   THAT'S IT. I'M SO OUTA HERE, I'M HALFWAY TO CHINA!

> *(He storms out.*
>
> *She is left looking after him.*
>
> *Try as she mentally does, he doesn't come back. From the longest silence possible, it is obvious he isn't coming back, either.*
>
> *She turns to an audience in her mind. She appeals powerlessly to it:)*

B: I know that, but…
> *(pause for one-liner effect, then fires at audience:)*

70

… WHY HE WANTS TO LEAVE ME, I'LL NEVER
KNOW!

*(She stays a moment for any reaction from the
audience, then turns and departs)*

(end)

I Know

Meat Axe on the Kitchen Door

(one-act play)

Meat Axe on the Kitchen Door

A one-act play for four actors.

In the residential home there is no peace while DAVID
and MUMPSIE are anywhere near each other. It is not so
much bickering but their outright, shouted abuse about
each other's family. Then there are the keepsakes that are
so precious to them, stored in the kit bag and wedding
travelling case that they can never take their eyes off.

And always, it seems, there is the meat axe hanging from
the kitchen door that one day... one fine day soon... they
might just have to resort to. It is a strange meat axe. It
does a lot of twirling in the air and bringing attention to
itself. Until it goes missing.

Cast
DAVID   resident of Home
MUMPSIE   older resident
THE MAN IN THE BLACK CLOAK
VIE   the resident's old hippie

Setting
No set scenery, except the 'hanging' image of the meat
axe on the kitchen door. This swims and sways – and
even comes and goes -- to dramatic effect.

The Home's TV lounge, the corridor, their rooms are
intimated by spot illumination.

Meat Axe on the Kitchen Door

(The meat axe hanging on the kitchen door is highlighted for a long moment on a darkened stage. It is heightened both in space and in illumination.

It starts, seemingly, to detach itself and then to sway back and forwards in mid-air. The light glints from its sharp edges.

DAVID emerges to stand 'before' it. He sways mesmerically with it for a long time. He only stops when MUMPSIE starts to swim into view, at which time he quickly stops and sinks back into the shadows.

MUMPSIE now fully emerges and stands 'before' the slowly swinging meat axe. She too sways with it mesmerically before she stops reluctantly and leaves.

The meat axe dissolves back to hanging on the kitchen door.

DAVID makes himself seen but remains shadowy. He is obviously a skulker, a secretive watcher of others, especially MUMPSIE until she 'departs'.

He does not fully emerge from the shadows even then, because VIE comes wandering absent-mindedly in. She resembles a distracted flower child of the Sixties with her floral flock and her

77

> *cock-feathered chapeau and her gleaming white*
> *Adidas runners.*

> *Around a clock strikes twelve midnight. It seems*
> *the signal for:)*

VIE: HEY! HEY! THE CHURCH BUS FLOAT BY?

> *(DAVID steps forward into the light. He obviously*
> *enjoys taunting her)*

DAVID: Whatareya?

VIE: Hey! Hey! You see the church bus floating by?

DAVID: (nastily) It's in the middle of the night, droopy-drawers. It's Wednesday.

VIE: (dreamily) I never know how the church bus knows that.

DAVID: Sag bum!

VIE: It went floating by?

DAVID: You all doubled up in the cardie, cock-eye.

VIE: Am I floating around with me cardie on going to church?

DAVID: (suddenly conspiratorially) You know what?

VIE: (alarmed) What?

(As THE MAN IN THE BLACK CLOAK half-appears off to one side, loomingly…)

DAVID: He said to me, he said, watchit Davy, it'll all come back.

VIE: (weird hope) The bus, will it?

DAVID: (ignoring her) He said don't muck it up, just think how I did it last time.

VIE: (suddenly, again) HEY! HEY! THE CHURCH BUS FLOAT BY?

DAVID: I said it's Wednesday not Sunday, dipstick.

(In response to that, VIE merely drops to the floor and sits there obstinately.

DAVID wants to taunt her further but has to quickly retreat into the shadows to watch all again, when MUMPSIE, in a greasy old nightie, emerges to help VIE.

MUMPSIE has trouble getting VIE to her feet, as much as she croons to the other old lady. It is not that VIE resists; it is just that she has gone limp.

While this is going on, DAVID, careful to keep to the shadows, approaches the form of THE MAN IN THE BLACK CLOAK as confidante:)

DAVID: She won't move. It's that Mumpsie, eh? She's waiting for me to muck up but I remember I've been through this before, too right. I know how the Americans ruined me last time, don't I?

Meat Axe on the Kitchen Door
> *(THE MAN IN BLACK CLOAK doesn't answer, but*
> *perhaps shrugs, perhaps nods. Whatever, it is*
> *enough encouragement for DAVID, who nods back*
> *conspiratorially and then steps back to watch*
> *MUMPSIE finally managing to get VIE to her feet*
> *and to lead her back to her room:)*

MUMPSIE: Cmon, cmon, old girl.

VIE: Waited for the bus, but it went floating by.

MUMPSIE: (real sympathy) I know, I know.

VIE: You shoulda seen it floating by.

MUMPSIE: You wouldn't read about it.

> *(As she is led off VIE degenerates in singing 'Little*
> *Baby Jesus' with made-up words without meaning.*

> *Sniggering, DAVID separates from THE MAN IN*
> *BLACK CLOAK and stands looking after the two*
> *women. He makes obviously derogatory motions*
> *about their going to the shadowy form, until:*

> *MUMPSIE returns hot under the collar. She does*
> *so from the other side of the stage, behind DAVID,*
> *and effectively startles him)*

MUMPSIE: I'M A MARRIED WOMAN!

> *(DAVID can only recover by appealing to the form*
> *of THE MAN IN THE BLACK CLOAK:)*

DAVID: Why's she always yelling abuse at me?

MUMPSIE: (standing ground) I'M A MARRIED WOMAN!

DAVID: (face boiling) NO YOU AIN'T!

MUMPSIE: I AM A MARRIED WOMAN, YOU!

DAVID: YOU'RE NOT MARRIED!

MUMPSIE: I AM!

DAVID: YOU'RE NOT! HE'S DEAD!

MUMPSIE: SO WHAT? I'M STILL MARRIED!

(THE MAN IN THE BLACK CLOAK speaks up for the first time, without leaving the shadows too much:)

MAN IN BLACK CLOAK: Ssh. Ssh.

(They instantly quieten, even though it isn't with too much grace.

MUMPSIE deliberately pushes past him, goes off to her room.

DAVID goes the other way.

He stops when he sees the meat axe hanging on the kitchen door again. He gets attuned to it, seems to throb as it throbs. Visually it seems to come down and to stop just out of his reach. Even so, without it, he makes slashing movements as though holding it. He does so towards where MUMPSIE has walked off)

81

Meat Axe on the Kitchen Door

DAVID: Take that, you stink!

(Light off him. The meat axe returns to hanging on the kitchen door.

Light on MUMPSIE, stopped outside her room. She too is looking at the meat axe and, too, seems to begin to throb when it seems to begin to throb. Again, it seems to descend to her, only to stop just short of her grasping hand.

Nevertheless, she too makes slashing movements with it against the direction of DAVID)

MUMPSIE: You're lucky, I tell you!

(A blackout like the blink of an eye.

When visibility comes back on it is from the light of a TV on. DAVID is holding the meat axe up to that light, making its sharp edge glint.

He chuckles.

THE MAN IN THE BLACK CLOAK comes near him)

MAN IN BLACK CLOAK: That feel good, does it?

DAVID: (affirming) Is this how I did it last time?

MAN IN BLACK CLOAK: It is definitely a pointer.

DAVID: I don't want to muck up.

(Light off him and next on MUMPSIE on other side of stage.

She too, in the light of the TV, is holding the meat axe and is fascinated by the light glinting off its sharp edges.

She chuckles.

THE MAN IN THE BLACK CLOAK appears near her)

MAN IN BLACK CLOAK: Does that feel good?

MUMPSIE: Watchit, don't let the legs go or they'll try to start climbing all over you.

MAN IN BLACK CLOAK: No.

MUMPSIE: Is this how I did it last time?

MAN IN BLACK CLOAK: It is definitely a pointer.

MUMPSIE: It's the legs that go first.

(An old-fashioned leather kit bag appears in its own light front and centre of the stage.

The lighting otherwise, including on the meat axe hanging on the kitchen door, fades behind it. As it does so, the voice of THE MAN IN BLACK CLOAK is heard trailing off:)

MAN IN BLACK CLOAK: It is definitely a pointer to the most precious thing of all your born days…

Meat Axe on the Kitchen Door
    (A silence follows this)

MAN IN BLACK CLOAK: Did you hear me?

DAVID: (breathlessly) Yes.

MUMPSIE: Yes.

> *(In the ensuing pause, there is a definitive time for
> the kit bag to become the solitary prop, and to
> become the centre of their attention)*

MAN IN THE BLACK CLOAK: See?

MUMPSIE: Yes.

DAVID: Yes.

> *(Slowly, the meat axe hanging on the kitchen door
> becomes re-illuminated up behind.*
>
> *Then the kit bag itself begins to glow in
> technicolour.*
>
> *First, DAVID re-emerges to almost full view to
> chuckle too forcibly over seeing it. And then he
> seems to gather boldness over creepiness, comes
> forward into the light, looking down on, and then
> kneeling down to, the kit bag.*
>
> *When he speaks, it is with rare positivity:)*

DAVID: I've had all this.

> *(THE MAN IN THE BLACK CLOAK appears at his
> side, as his insinuating Iago)*

84

MAN IN BLACK CLOAK: Of course you have.
>   *(then)*
But not your kit bag. Not this here bag, the one they promised you, so I hear.

DAVID: No friggin' way!

MAN IN BLACK CLOAK: No. Little wonder how pretty it is. Little wonder.

DAVID: Little wonder, what?

MAN IN BLACK CLOAK: All the pretty colours of the most precious thing in all your born days that had been promised.

DAVID: Promised too right!

MAN IN BLACK CLOAK: (affirming) Promised. Your kit bag, not the born days. Ah, the born days…

DAVID: (nodding) Locked away real safe in there just for me.

MAN IN BLACK CLOAK: What are they?

DAVID: Things before I could much remember, like.

>   *(THE MAN IN THE BLACK CLOAK stops and somehow orchestrates from the other:)*

DAVID: It brings…

Meat Axe on the Kitchen Door

MAN IN BLACK CLOAK: (prompting) It brings tears to his eye, your eye, what he or you or you-or-he has been made to miss…

DAVID: (keyed on) It brings tears to his eye, what he has been made to miss all his born days, stuff it. He remembers the judge telling him your mother left you at birth for the State he has come to realize has to mean the United States of America, don't you worry about that.

MAN IN BLACK CLOAK: What else?

DAVID: (nodding, carrying on) And he remembers how the judge…

MAN IN BLACK CLOAK: … in that black cloak…

DAVID: (nodding) … that judge in that black cloak must have told the Americans to lock his childish things away in the kitbag for safekeeping until he was ready old enough to collect it. Right?

MAN IN BLACK CLOAK: It sounds like all of childhood.

DAVID: It sounds like all of childhood, yep.

MAN IN BLACK CLOAK: Right you are.

DAVID: Bloody oath it was right! The judge, he told him right off, he said: They shouldn't have left me alone at birth…

MAN IN BLACK CLOAK: Was it 'me' and was it 'he'?

DAVID: Not half it wasn't! And he told them the States shouldn't have left me alone to go to school. They shouldn't have left him alone in all those shops. They should have had some surveillance that might have stopped me.

MAN IN THE BLACK CLOAK: You were saying about the kit bag…?

DAVID: He said that what they do in the States of. He said the boy has to pack up his dreams in my old kit bag and smile smile smile. He said I was not to open it until I got to the stage I didn't muck up as to how I can do it last time.

MAN IN BLACK CLOAK: The last time…?

DAVID: Like how I did it last time!

MAN IN BLACK CLOAK: (seductively) And did that boy learn how he did it last time?

DAVID: (unsure) You bet.

MAN IN BLACK CLOAK: And did you muck up?

DAVID: (evasive, shrewdly) The thing is just relax and let it come back to you, see
        (then almost into air, certainly towards the meat
        axe hanging on the kitchen door; hiss:)
How do you know about my kit bag?

MAN IN BLACK CLOAK: We have our pens; and we have our papers.

87

Meat Axe on the Kitchen Door
> *(and then, pointing, as the kit bag fades from
> DAVID's view)*

MAN IN BLACK CLOAK: But where is it, your famous
kit bag with all your precious live-long days?

DAVID: (outcry) IT'S IN HER ROOM!

MAN IN BLACK CLOAK: Ah, that's the rub, isn't it?

> *(He disappears. The kit bag has disappeared.*
>
> *DAVID, forlorn, looks down at his hands. He is
> holding the meat axe.*
>
> *Blackout.*
>
> *A quick return to spot, where, again, the bag is
> front and centre of stage and throbbing colours of
> the rainbow seductively.*
>
> *On the other side of the stage, with the MAN IN
> THE BLACK CLOAK 'Iago-like' to her too,
> MUMPSIE emerges to stand over, and to kneel to,
> the bag very longingly. Finally:)*

MUMPSIE: I've had all this.

MAN IN BLACK CLOAK: (insinuating) Of course you
have.
> *(then)*
But not your wedding travelling case. Not this bag here,
so I hear.

MUMPSIE: Never!

MAN IN BLACK CLOAK: No. Little wonder how pretty it is. Little wonder.

MUMPSIE: (sleepily) Little wonder, what?

MAN IN BLACK CLOAK: All the pretty colours of the most precious thing in all your born days that has been promised.

MUMPSIE: Promised.

MAN IN BLACK CLOAK: (affirming) Promised. Your wedding travelling case, not the born days. Ah, the born days...

> (He stops and, as he did to DAVID, orchestrates
> from the other:)

MUMPSIE: It brings...

MAN IN BLACK CLOAK: (prompting) It brings tears to her eyes, what she or you or you-or-she has been made to bear...
> (she nods)
They wouldn't think to speak in such blackness with those few pins of lights of what might happen up ahead, fearful for all women.

MUMPSIE: Watchit, watchit. Don't let the old legs go or they try climbing all over you.

MAN IN BLACK CLOAK: Who're they?

MUMPSIE: All the rotten things! Nobody's going to throw their leg over me! 'Ere, you can smell him! Ash all over him and how he stinks.

(she spits)

MAN IN BLACK CLOAK: Who might that be?

MUMPSIE: That David, who else? Stinking rotten with tobacco. How would you be, mothering that? She doesn't care why he thinks he can shout at her all the time; she won't lie down to abuse like that.

MAN IN BLACK CLOAK: Is it 'she' or 'you'?

MUMPSIE: (just carries on) She doesn't care why he thinks he can shout at her all time; I won't lie down to abuse like that. That trying to shout her down, on about her poor husband; she's never let anyone climb all over her and I'm not starting now!
(and)
You know what I think?

MAN IN BLACK CLOAK: What, Mumpsie?

MUMPSIE: They let them in straight out of the gutter these days.

> *(She looks down. She has the meat axe shining in her hand. She waves it around protectively, pretend fighting. She looks down. It isn't in her hand any more.*
>
> *THE MAN IN THE BLACK CLOAK understands, nods. She quietens)*

 MUMPSIE: (surly) I can't even go near that kitchen. I shouldn't have come to this at my age. Thank the Lord my God I've got my legs but I should never have got to know where they hang that vicious-looking weapon on the kitchen door. Trying to climb all over me.

MAN IN BLACK CLOAK: But doesn't Mumpsie still stumble on, hmm?

MUMPSIE: (nodding) Trying her level best. She continues to grope the walls to feel her way in the dark. Why am I always the one they come to when someone's in strife, having to feel me way in the dark? How can anyone get some shuteye with that filthy reeking animal and his television going all hours of the night?

> *(THE MAN IN THE BLACK CLOAK brings her attention back to the kit bag)*

MAN IN BLACK CLOAK: You'd think she should keep her eye on her wedding travelling case.

> *(She is obviously relieved from anxiety to have her attention brought back to it. She moves to it, clasps her hands in joy above it)*

MAN IN BLACK CLOAK: And the purity veil.

MUMPSIE: (softly now) And the purity veil.

MAN IN BLACK CLOAK: And the dance of the virgins.

MUMPSIE: What I was once.
> *(then)*

Watchit, keep the old legs going. They go first, and then they all think they got some right to start climbing all over you.

Meat Axe on the Kitchen Door

MAN IN BLACK CLOAK: (again) And your wedding travelling case and your purity veil…?

MUMPSIE: (dreamishly) As usual, she moves down the long dark corridor, circling, ducking, hhhrrrrmmm goes the electricity in the dark of night, see, and oh how it breaks out into the light until… until…

MAN IN BLACK CLOAK: Until… you or she, you and she…?

MUMPSIE: Until she sees her border collie, my Fetch… hello, Fetch, Fetch, go Fetch, hello… and it's her younger time, isn't it?, and how it's sweeping its lovely golden-browns across the sweeping green of the cricket field to explode all the skies in and around me with the purity veil of the dancing gulls. Yes, oh yes. And in that moment, I knew the purity veil was being pulled soft, soft across her face, soft as purity, as it always will be for her live-long, as ever long as she has legs to reach it, her wedding travelling case of mine.
(catches breath; kneels by the case)
In it… they called it my wedding travelling case, you know… are… are… well…

(She touches her nose for a secret, but he is leaning over her now and:)

MAN IN BLACK CLOAK: … are the most precious things of her life live safe. Things quiet and still and full of confetti. Time of the sweet virginity wall. The purity veil of the virgin.

MUMPSIE: 'The purity veil of the virgin'. I like that.

MAN IN BLACK CLOAK: (adding) The things smiling
at her as the purity veil comes down to stroke her face.

MUMPSIE: (quietly) That's right.
   (then stronger)
But I'll be alright while my legs hold out good.
   (and)
How did you know about my wedding travelling case?

MAN IN BLACK CLOAK: We have our pens; and we
have our papers.

   *(and then, pointing, as the kit bag fades from before
   her very eyes and she can't prevent it from doing
   so:)*

MAN IN BLACK CLOAK: But where is it, your
wedding travelling case with your purity veil?

MUMPSIE: (outcry) IT'S IN HIS ROOM!

MAN IN BLACK CLOAK: Ah, that's the rub, isn't it?

   (Blackout.

   *In a brief interim the meat axe glows even more
   from its hook on the kitchen door)*

MAN IN BLACK CLOAK: See how that thing glows?

MUMPSIE: Yes.

DAVID: Yes.

   (The meat axe begins to pulse, seemingly sway.

Meat Axe on the Kitchen Door
> *Into their separated spots re-emerge DAVID and*
> *MUMPSIE. They start swaying with the pulsing of*
> *the meat axe. It is palpably alluring.*

> *Renewed blackout)*

2.

> *(DAVID and MUMPSIE are back 'slinking' in the*
> *shadows on either side of the stage.*

> *THE MAN IN THE BLACK CLOAK is openly*
> *centre, trying to pull them in)*

MAN IN BLACK CLOAK: What are we going to say to each other now?

> *(He gets only answering angry shifts in the*
> *darkness on either side)*

MAN IN BLACK CLOAK: I think we should say something to each other now that we seem to have lost the meat axe that was hanging on the kitchen door, don't you?
> *(and)*
Any ideas?

> *(They throw accusations across the stage)*

DAVID: I know who the thief is.

MUMPSIE: I know who the thieving thief is.

MAN IN BLACK CLOAK: That's precisely why we should say something to each other, don't you reckon?

(Gets a loud raspberry from either side)

MAN IN BLACK CLOAK: Now, with the meat axe missing, we don't want to go all silly, do we?

MUMPSIE: (emerging, ready for a fight) He started it.

DAVID: (ditto) She started it.

MAN IN BLACK CLOAK: Did the police search your rooms too? I think they did.

MUMPSIE: Yeah, and I told 'em: If you don't keep a lookout, your legs go first and then they start having a go at climbing all over you!

DAVID: (bettering her) Yeah, an' I gave it to them straight out, I said: I only have to think how I did it last time, don't I? They said are you talking about the missing meat axe, and I said hey I'm talking about not mucking up.

MUMPSIE: Same here, with bells on.
    *(then rather surprising accusation at THE MAN IN
    THE BLACK CLOAK)*
You promised you'd do something about him.

DAVID: (ditto again) Yeah, you promised you'd do something about her.

MAN IN BLACK CLOAK: That's a bit rich, don't you reckon.

Meat Axe on the Kitchen Door

MUMPSIE: I know when I need to piddle. I've got a right to piddle. I've got a right to be able to go for a piddle without knowing he's going to be lurking around in that TV glow of his, skulking just outside my door. I know he's got a meat axe dangling at his side, as though he's all innocence, ha.

DAVID: HA TO YOU!

MUMPSIE: HA TO YOU!

DAVID: I've got a right to get up and switch on the TV. I like watching TV in the middle of the night. I'm allowed to like the TV lounge when it's not smelling of old ladies' pee without having to creep around knowing she's doing that old creepy thing with that meat axe dangling by her side, ready to use.

MUMPSIE: Don't think I'm scared of him. I just know how your legs can go sudden-like and then they start trying to climb all over you.

DAVID: I know it's no use mucking up until you remember how you did it last time, like. That's what *I* know.

> *(THE MAN IN THE BLACK CLOAK simply disappears suddenly.*
>
> *When both of them simultaneously look down, they see they have the meat axe in their hands.*
>
> *With these raised aggressively they circle each other.)*

MUMPSIE: DON'T YOU TRY AND CLIMB ALL OVER ME!

DAVID: YOUR FAMILY WON'T EVEN LOOK AT YOU, OLD FART!

MUMPSIE: I'LL CLOBBER YOU ONE!

DAVID: THEY'RE NOT STUPID LIKE YOU. THEY WON'T HAVE A BAR OF YOU!

MUMPSIE: OH YEAH, SO WHY DO THEY STILL WANT TO LIVE WITH ME, SMARTY PANTS?!

DAVID: BULLSHIT!

MUMPSIE: BULLSH TO YOU, TOO!

> *(THE MAN IN THE BLACK CLOAK reappears again as suddenly as he disappeared.*
>
> *They are not disappointed he has returned to keep the peace; in fact they seem to have been waiting for it.*
>
> *He claps his hands to stop it, but not alarmingly. It's as usual; that they both recognize his kindly voice kindly come and not a moment too soon:)*

MAN IN BLACK CLOAK: Ssh. Go to bed now.
  (but cautionary first)
Show me your hands first.

> *(David hides the meat axe behind his back knowing it's not there anymore.*

Meat Axe on the Kitchen Door
　　Mumpsie hides the meat axe behind her back
　　knowing it's not there anymore.

　　They both hide the meat axe still hanging on the
　　kitchen door and return to their rooms feeling they
　　haven't mucked up.

　　After they have gone, he is every bit the Night
　　Nurse:)

MAN IN BLACK CLOAK: Good night.

　　(He withdraws.

　　But DAVID and MUMPSIE creep back. When they
　　do so, the meat axe hanging on the kitchen door
　　starts spinning in the air between them.

　　It spins and thrums like a whirling dervish, like a
　　wild diamond in the sky.

　　They make grabs at it but miss. And then it, and
　　they, fade.

　　Blackout renewed.

　　In the blackness, comes a dim (could be candle)
　　light on one side and then the other as:)

MAN IN BLACK CLOAK: David?

DAVID: I only have to think how I did it last time, don't
I?

MAN IN BLACK CLOAK: Yes.

DAVID: The Americans ruined me last time. See, everyone knows me now, so I can't muck up.

MAN IN BLACK CLOAK: The judge's even coming to see you pretty soon not mucking up, I promise.

DAVID: Tell him I'm not letting him down, no sir. Tell him I've still got my kitbag he gave me. We might even share a look-see inside, eh?

MAN IN BLACK CLOAK: Really?

DAVID: No sweat.

MAN IN BLACK CLOAK: David, what did you steal?

DAVID: (gleefully) *I stole her room key!*

MAN IN BLACK CLOACK: Ssh. Go to bed.

(The dim light switches to the other side, where:)

MAN IN BLACK CLOAK: Mumpsie.

MUMPSIE: You have to watch it or your legs go first.

MAN IN BLACK CLOAK: I know.

MUMPSIE: Keep a secret about what the best medicine of all is?

MAN IN BLACK CLOAK: Okay.

MUMPSIE: If it wasn't for my wedding travelling case, I'd be flat out on my back long ago with 'em trying to

Meat Axe on the Kitchen Door
make my legs go first. Best is the purity veil. Best ever.
When the old legs were closed, like. You want to try it.

MAN IN BLACK CLOAK: But you're not flat out.

MUMPSKIE: Not now, I'm not. No one's going to
throw their leg over me.

MAN IN BLACK CLOAK: So what did you steal?

MUMPSIE: (gleefully) *I stole his room key!*

MAN IN BLACK CLOAK: Ssh. Go to bed.

> *(Blackout.*
>
> *After this, the central area is lit. It is the middle of
> the night.*
>
> *In the centre of the lit area is the bag, glowing
> technicolour again.*
>
> *First, it is DAVID who comes in and, in a danse
> macabre, furtively circles around the bag in
> narrowing circles.*
>
> *Unseen by him and equally not seeing him,
> MUMPSIE follows. She does her own danse
> macabre – furtive and in narrowing circles -- but in
> the opposite direction.*
>
> *Each has the meat axe in their hand.*
>
> *Now, in that glow of cunning, David has gained his
> kitbag at last. He does not need light. He has*

*always known where his kitbag of his childhood
would exactly be.*

*He feels, yes, the thrill of kneeling at his own
wanted place at last.*

*The kitbag is locked but with the thrill at first he
does not panic that it resists the point of the meat
axe in his hand. Straining and gouging with it, he
tries hard to remember, yet still cannot think, how
some other screwdriver or other has already
gouged and clawed the locks until he realizes there
must have been some other last time.*

*In the panic that comes from that realization, he
strikes with the meat axe blindly. Then he strikes
out again and again with the meat axe, until he has
found unimaginatively that he has burst the old
leather through.*

*The thrill he can evidently feel. He pushes his hand
in through the leather of it; he gropes for what has
been in promise of safe-keeping for him from his
best childhood days for all of his born days. What
the judge said. What the judge promised all those
years ago – for the States to lock his childhood
away for safekeeping until he knew he was ready
from the last time.*

He finds nothing.

*He tries again, grabbing around the sides, around
the ups and downs of it.*

There is nothing in there. In there, is nothing.

101

Meat Axe on the Kitchen Door
   He screams silently and scrambles back.

Now it is the turn of MUMPSIE.

*She has completed her danse macabre and,
mindless of him, not seeing him, she too goes
through the triumph of finding her wedding
travelling case at last – and then having to fight to
break in to it with the point of her meat axe.*

*And when she has managed to do so, she too
plunges her hand into it, only to find it unbelievably
empty.*

*In her madness of finding it like this, she tries to
wrench it away.*

*This is at the point when DAVID tries to wrench his
bag of childhood away.*

They tug-of-war over the bag.

*THE MAN IN THE BLACK CLOAK appears above
them. He is physically and mentally 'over all' and:)*

MAN IN BLACK CLOACK: As usual he feels he has
lost his childhood again and all the good things the judge
promised the States of America would give him if only he
was ready like the last time if he could forget that it never
came.
   (and)
As usual she has gone crazy watching the border collie
called Fetch, do Fetch, of her old time sweep its lovely
colours across the cricketing greens to douse her mind of
lost'n'losing virginities with the purity veil of the
exploding gulls.

(and)

And, as the high night wanes, while he is screaming silently before her, she feels how she cannot stop the hot intimacy of her own blood rive down her cheeks. She tastes much of it and finds it warmly her own and not so good. It is strange how her meat axe is in his meat axe and how it is swinging against herself in heavy chunks and how her meat axe is swinging against his head in heavy chunks and he feels how he cannot stop the hot intimacy of his own blood roll down his cheeks and tastes much of it and finds it warm and not so good. She finds it strange to be looking at last down into her secret wedding case, in which has always kept safe and sound her dear husband and dear children and yet, after all the wait for his-and-her waking and wedding dream, they are not bursting into the purity veil of the exploding gulls she is offering from all her skies and he is finding it strange he is not bursting with a roiling of childhood come at last as the States had promised, as the old judge had promised.

(voice risen to absolute certainly above them)

There is nothing as much as the blood rives. Empty. In there, there is nothing. It is as though they have gone missing. In there, is nothing.

> *(Confused, David stares down at the empty space of his childhood they had promised would be in keepsake.*
>
> *Confused, Mumpsie stares down at the empty space where she had secretly kept her family safe and sound and in virginity's purity veil.*
>
> *Both shout into the air simultaneously:)*

DAVID AND MUMPSIE: YOU'VE KILLED ME!

Meat Axe on the Kitchen Door

MAN IN BLACK CLOAK: (laughing) I WAS JUST KIDDING!

(Blackout.

When next lighting is up, it is the fading light of the next evening.

THE MAN IN THE BLACK CLOAK... the Night Nurse... is softly rebuking them:)

MAN IN BLACK CLOAK: You know it's a no go running around at night trying to spook each other out. It's not how a mother and son behave.

DAVID: SHE AIN'T MY MOTHER!

MUMPSIE: HE'S NOT MY SON!

MAN IN THE BLACK CLOAK: Oh, you big kidders, you.   What we want both of you to do is relax and let it come back to you, how you did it last time, hmm?'

(Into this, VIE comes. She is dressed as at the beginning... with her floral dress and chapeau and Adidas runners. She is ready for church but cannot find where to go:)

VIE: HEY! HEY! THE CHURCH BUS FLOAT BY?

(end)

The New Councillor's Inaugural Speech

(short play)

The New Councillor's Inaugural Speech

A short play/workshop cut-and-thrust.

Lisabeth Getem-Kraken comes back local as Boroondara's new member of the city council from her United Nations and Commonwealth Secretariat roles. She wants only for the people of her new electorate to know they need not be agasp to opening their borders to gulps of air, pure and simple.

The New Councillor's Inaugural Speech

Cast
PUBLICITY OFFICER
THE NEW COUNCILLOR
Optional: Various appreciative and non-appreciative listeners

Setting
A podium and two chairs behind. Maybe a council flag stuck up behind. On the podium itself is a print out that reads 'Cr. Lisabeth Getem-Kraken'

108

The New Councillor's Inaugural Speech

(At the podium, the PUBLICITY OFFICER is midway into his introduction, or at least pretending he is:)

PUBLICITY OFFICER: … If you can ever nail down the URL of the Council you've lost the name of, then the following navigation might help you further on the website you can't find: go the tab 'Home', then to 'Your Council' top right, then follow link to 'Media Releases' and then 'November'.
(and)
That's November of this year. How do I know? Because it's now, of course, ha ha. If you don't find anything under 'November', then I'd suggest waiting a suitable time to allow now to pass and try again. Never know your luck in the big city, right?
(starts up again)
So, as I say, her eagerly awaited speech is entitled 'On a Whiff of a Prayer; Gasping the Nettle of Local Development'. A transcript will be prepared when a new Spellchecker gets through Finance.
(and)
With that a-do, it is my pleasure to bring you Councillor Lisabeth Getem-Kraken. Councillor Lisabeth Getem-Kraken brings international expertise to your Council, especially as a conservationist who wouldn't stand still and local-government specialist with The Commonwealth Secretariat.
(flourish)

The New Councillor's Inaugural Speech

This expertise came to the fore on the occasion of her maiden speech to the Council, when she tabled the transcript of the speech she gave to the Fifth Commonwealth Local Government Conference, rather than address the Council itself and so add unnecessarily to the debate on overblown human carbon emissions and whether they were worth having in your face. (My opinion wasn't asked, but can be traced.) At the Commonwealth Secretariat she had special responsibility for the overall analysis of expiration dates. She is married with four children, who were brought up, and pertaining to which plus other things, she says:

(read quote)

'on the fundamental human rights principle that a breath gained is a proper airing given'.

('back' again)

Need we say more? So, with that selfsame a-do, I part the seas, ha ha. Ladies and gentlemen, our new councillor Lisabeth Getem-Kraken...

(He makes way for her in a usual exchange of places at the podium.

She quietens the applause she obviously hears)

COUNCILLOR GRETEM-KRAKEN: Good afternoon. I have great pleasure in welcoming our conference partners in the Commonwealth Local Government Forum*, especially the Association of Local Governments of Australia which represents all 675 local living-and-breathing councils here and of course to our hosts the Clean Air City of Nasal Melbourne...

(The PUBLICITY OFFICER blithely interrupts, leaning over to the mikes)

110

PUBLICITY OFFICER: In needed, please read instead here 'Welcome to my fellow councillors at this Spring carnival meeting of the Boroondara City Council.

(goes to withdraw, but:)

Oh, and please use the pens provided to fill in your own area if you have access to a website that features this facility.

(She has to nudge him aside)

COUNCILLOR GETEM-KRAKEN: Fellow... thingmabobs, I would like to commence on a personal note, if I may. Given the global issues of climate change, I am reminded of the late-2013 bushfires which led to a state of emergency in my second cousin's home town of Omeo in the slopes of eastern Victoria. As a result, my family and the unprecedented population of over 263 were held in a breathless state for ten whole days. The fires came within a few hundred metres and, for safety reasons, along with that of the horses and cattle, plus all the air breathing pigs, we moved to the coast where breathing restrictions had not come into place. I observed then at firsthand how communities come together in the face of potential breathing disasters that, in my humble opinion, all branches of science, including shared ethics, ignore at their own peril. And maybe that should even be at 'its' own peril.

(goes on)

At the time of these lung-scorching fires, I had already spent almost a decade researching rural communities trying to understand why and how they were successful at turning individual breathing into a shared survival. This frontline ability to deal with adversity I call community breathing. It refers to a locally collective reaction that deals with breathing in such a way that any adverse reaction to breathing is minimised until the threat of not

111

breathing is over. Threats can be natural breathing disasters like said bushfires or tornados but they can also be things such as community breathless moments or situations such as mine disasters under which the whole process of breathing can come under strain.

(larger breath)

The Morwell mining region had long ago sprang to my mind as an ideal location to study this breathing resiliency. For example, in the long mining history of the region, there have been hundreds of mining accidents in which over 99.99% have resulted in breathing deficiencies that have, in turn, become a major social challenge for the people of Morwell to face. I began to talk to people there to find out why they thought the community had been able to breathe through all these events. Furthermore, I did control studies with neighbouring communities that had also experienced breathing which might indicate non-mining breathing activity. One of these communities had dealt with the possible development of a large scale breathing learning institute in their vicinity, resulting in a costly ten-year battle with authorities and costing the community a lot of wasted breath. An important point here was that it created tensions between those who wanted the new breathing technosciences and those who wanted to stick to the traditional ways of pulling things in. Needless to say, either party was either mightily vocal or extremely throaty. Other communities between the mining and non-mining sectors talked about the stress they were under due to breathing taking the middle path. They reported being so small they found themselves being starved of oxygen.

(pause for effect)

So what might we learn from these communities and their breathing experiences? Firstly, community breathing is a process that all communities strive to gain mastery of, and that this aspiration fluctuates over time. Secondly, sometimes communities can handle breathing more successfully than others depending upon outside influences allowing new populations to have breathing space – or, I should add, suffering a net loss due to mortality and youth-depreciation and the like. Thirdly, it is very important that the community develop positive breathing techniques in order to develop a sense of belonging. Fourthly, this leads to creating a sense of community or of sharing a useful activity as a binding activity without lung leakages. Finally, people feel more community-bonded if they are encouraged to help their neighbours during breathing alerts. A common example given to me was to follow what happened on maternity beds.

(The PUBLICITY OFFICER jumps in)

PUBLICITY OFFICER: Some of you may be wondering about maternity beds here.

(In a 'they-may-not' way, she elbows him aside and continues:)

COUNCILLOR GETEM-KRAKEN: It is crucial that residents are proactive; anticipating what breath lies ahead of them by preparing themselves for breathing as an inevitable process. I have called this breathing resiliency. Breathing resiliency depends heavily upon having visionary leadership in breathing techniques supported by greater State investment in the area, especially in the aspirations of minority groups. When all this is in place, patterns of breathing should become discernible such that plans can be formulated for early-warning systems to counter Nature's inevitable out-of-breath ructions as a force of gasp we have to suffer. It is also in times like those that we learn how much a

113

community relies on its past breaths, facing the fact that
the last one isn't necessarily the last one. This doesn't
mean that all residents will be happy with the breath they
take. But for the majority, a better breathing process
should result in their community being better able to
endure through the direct path of their nostrils.

(pause to look around)

Of course, my conclusions posed a core problem for the
UN Framework Convention on Climate Change – that is,
why is breathing important if it is interfering with the
CO_2 emissions? I believe a community with inherent
breathing resiliency has a greater chance of sustaining
breath in the long run. I also believe there are people we
are able to turn to help make this breath happen on a
regular basis. Health and social service providers can
work with rural residents to help their communities
overcome ignorance of breathing. Ways to do this
include: developing breathing demonstrations that foster
the use of the body's own breathing tube as an aid;
building breathing resources and nostril capillary
capacities; and working with communities to sort out
what they want to accomplish with the breathing they
already have. Breathing builds on the strengths of rural
communities -- and retaining local residents is its greatest
guarantee of being fostering a healthy sector. Sustainable-
breathing communities, or, as I call them, SBCs, mean a
stronger society. If a future, there lies oxygenation! We
have only to turn upon our respirators!

(pause division obviously needed)

I would now like to turn from the personal to the broader
multinational issues of the atmospheres we have to
operate in. In exercising our breathing rights, no country
is an eerie. One might speculate that the future of
breathing is no longer a case of pie-in-the-sky aeromancy.
The United Nations itself, through UNCED, adopted
Agenda 21; the UN Framework Convention on Air

Climate Change (UNFCACC); the Convention on
Breathing Biodiversity Light (COBBLE); and a Statement
of Principles on the sustainable use and management of
lungs and/or chlorophyll systems in the not-so-
respiratorial (NSRs). It also set in motion negotiations
that led to new agreements on nasal filtration under
desertification, migratory air stocks, and the sustainability
of so-called de rigueur breathing regimes in small states,
starting from what is escaping from the side of mouths in
froth-form is often pure oxygen wasted.
   (stern change of tone)
Yet many Commonwealth developing countries,
especially the Least Aerobic Countries (LACs) less able
to cope with the cycle of inflation in and deflation out,
inflation in and deflation out etcetera...

   (The PUBLICITY OFFICER jumps in undeniably)

PUBLICITY OFFICER: Excuse me, Councillor.
   (to gathering)
We decided here to take the poetic license of spelling
'etcetera' as its diminutive 'etc' or spelling the diminutive
'etc' as its extended seven-letter older cousin 'etcetera'.
We held our breath for a long time over this, but... well...
there you are.

   *(steps aside with reluctance and a shrug of the
   shoulders)*

COUNCILLOR GETEM-KRAKEN: (long-suffering
return) ...inflation in and deflation out, 'etcetera', lack the
capacity to suspire effectively during such negotiations or,
indeed, to keep abreast of all the issues nation-building
breathing exercises clearly outlined in wall charts in
gymnasia all over the world sans borders and schools with
walls. You might recognise this as the classic gasp-and-

clasp syndrome. The Commonwealth Secretariat provides support to help these countries keep breathing in and out in self-supporting ways. Even so, advisory work on the development of legal and policy guidelines to ensure international agencies get to the bottom of lung capacities at the national level would seem to require, frankly, less throat clearing and more talk. Hot air is a killer of people with a tendency towards overheating of their sinuses, as I know too well.

PUBICITY OFFICER: (jumping in) See Fifth Assessment Report or FAR, IPCC Working Group II; turn the pages until it matters....

(She throws a look of daggers at him but continues:)

COUNCILLOR GETEM-KRAKEN: At all times, I think we should all remind ourselves that there resides an underlying principle for all of us – and that is there can never be any life after breath unless you possess the capacity to use your lungs.
(pause)
Lastly, I would like to touch on the legal and regulatory breathing spaces concerning the obligations of small states under the various environmental conventions to counter oxygen deficiency -- a condition I am wont to call Societal Hypoxyia – and to complement respiration. The Commonwealth Secretariat also sensitized air-locked and geographically-vacuumed states (Swaziland, December 2004) on the rights accorded them by the 1982 United Nations Convention on the Law of the Air -- especially on access to oxygenic particles, sharing of surplus breathing stockpiles through Exclusive Aeronomic Zones, and maintenance of all deep air recesses. This over-riding Convention encourages those states to enter into buddy-

breathing protocols such as that advocated by Dive Australia, with states in oxygen-desperate states given full rights to a good old-fashion suck and keep sucking until someone tells you to stop or says 'of the old sav'.

(finally)

Finally, I think we should all reflect on how one exhalation held off is extinction forever and how we cannot hold our breath while waiting for the future just to blow over us. It is not easy, nor intended to be, to watch your own chest rising and falling.

(and)

I thank you all very much. And I can tell you the first thing I'm going to do now is find out what Arab walked out of these chambers and left the door open. I am not a fan of draughts. Nor should any of us be. It is up to us, every one of us. We can either open our borders or close them... open or close them... open or close... open and close... in and out, in and out. It need not be our last dry gulp. Again, thank you all very much.

(Steps away finally.

The PUBLICITY OFFICER is not one to miss out on the last word:)

PUBLICITY OFFICER: For 'I thank you all very much', please consider the alternative which very nearly got passed by a majority instead of being lost unanimously: 'Mr Mayor, Councillors, guests in the public gallery, and all those of Cougham ward who vented for me but still couldn't blow me off track, without their help of which'. Sentence will end properly later.

(end)

The New Councillor's Inaugural Speech

The New Councillor's Augural Speech

(short play)

Monologue/workshopper.

It is the new Councillor's second and most augural speech since her inaugural speech. With the rise of the populist sentiment in the country's politics, she is fearless in aiming the barbs and arrows of her logic straight at the heart of Australia's Aboriginal problem – the rise of the *vox populi.*

Cast
THE NEW COUNCILLOR
THE PUBLICITY OFFICER
Optional: various appreciative and non-appreciative listeners

Setting
Once more, the podium and two chairs behind. Maybe a council flag stuck up behind. On the podium itself is the same print out that reads 'Cr. Lisabeth Getem-Kraken'

The New Councillor's Augural Speech

(The PUBLICITY OFFICER is at the podium and is decidedly grumpy and certainly essentially unaccommodating.)

PUBLICITY OFFICER: All right, loosen up and belt up. Yeah, I know that's a contradiction in terms, but anyone who knows me well… and, thank God, there's not one of you here who knows me well… would know that this last week has been a really shitty week for me. It's frankly not right that I should be asked to do my job and introduce our new Councillor for the second time.
(to a heckle)
Yeah, yeah, I get paid for it. And that's not right, but who listens to me?
(to nobody obviously listening)
I said, who listens to me?
(to another heckle)
'Transcript', shitbum there says. This is Australia, mate. You get the literacy rate up and then we'll think about getting transcripts and raising local government rates. You lot be satisfied with what our own 'Boroondara International Tribune' said after last week, and it pains me to have to read, and I quote:
(reads from newspaper clipping)
'Inside the city council chamber, the other councillors broke and, other than the inaugural speaker, the new Councillor Lisabeth Getem-Kraken, said they had to desperately go outside to get their hands around but expressed not what. Tea proved hard to find. Not one,

other than the new Councillor, made that scheduled evening session for further discussion. However, when they arrived the next day, they found Cr Lisabeth Getem-Kraken had not moved from her place, no sir, nor even, it is said, sat. She understood about the tea but her constituency demanded she made a constituency before she stormed out of the chamber making a rude noise on her constituents' behalf. If her vocal cords had any life left in them, they wouldn't be coming back. It was plain her international experience had better things to do. A morning cup of tea for a start. There were apparently no notes left for the Council Minutes. The new councillor was heard stating she preferred to let her speech speak for itself.'

COUNCILLOR GETEM-KRAKEN: (from her chair at back) I certainly did!

PUBLICITY OFFICER: Thank you, Councillor Getem-Kraken, for the need to say no more.
(carries on)
I might add: re that newspaper article I just read out. That had nothing to do with me. I just wrote it.
(then)
On a personal note, the subject of our newest councillor's speech today happens to be one the dearest to my heart. It is entitled 'Speaking for the Lost Generations; or, When the Mouth Opens, a Few Future Jaws Will Drop' – and I refuse to listen to a word of it!

(He huffs off.

The new councillor is left to wait until it is obvious he is not returning, then to shrug, get up and approach the podium on her lonesome. She is quite happy to do so.)

COUNCILLOR GETEM-KRAKEN: Good morning. I
will not hum nor ha for I know how important it is to
speak plainly on this subject of national importance
before the next tea break.
(pause)
To repeat, the subject of this talk is: 'Speaking for the
Lost Generations; or, When the Mouth Opens, a Few
Future Jaws Will Drop'… a bit of a mouthful, I admit.
(settles into:)
Vocalising abuse and neglect among the human race is
not new. In the nineteenth century those advocating for
the maltreated were called 'the sound biters'. They tried
to help communities change from seeing humans as slugs,
snails, and the slimier like who or that are unable to make
any sort of meaningful sound outside of various traction
squeaks to fully-formed creatures with sounds to voice
and words to give.
(pause)
Nowadays there are entrenched groups even within us
who work on the impulse of admitting words into society,
but who still remain the objects of verbal abuse. From our
early economic migrants to the first people in Australia
who could form the sounds to say 'Aboriginal, bub' –
who anthropologists have dubbed 'The Mouthy
Australians' -- we are finally learning about the painful
experiences of sounds kept warehoused in voice boxes no
bigger than a solitary-confinement cell in old Pentridge
Gaol where many of those voice boxes unfortunately
ended up. However, the removal policies in relation to
such pent-up sound and voices, and perhaps even words
of Aboriginal or non-Aboriginal descent, remain one of
the heaviest calls to arms for our nation, especially in the
total lack of such removal policies from a surgical point
of view. Very few of us, I venture to say, have witnessed

a humanlike sound set free or an unfettered word on the loose.

(pause)

The State in loco mentis parenthesis seems to have nothing but silence to say on this atrocity, though all of us know how many have demanded a simple sound – that is, two sounds -- like sorry, let alone five sounds like I apologise. Without citing words or sighting sounds, we are confined to ask in a terrible vacuum how any State can perform the functions of an encouraging society to rise up against its grip on words. These are not idle words, either. Very recent US research suggests that many voice boxes stolen by society are moved from foster voice boxees to foster voice boxees without anyone thus voice-boxed at a tender age getting a word in edgeways... and most of them do so without a word being said let alone that edgeways, while those left to remain in the familiar circumstances of the one foster family, or voice boxers, have been known to more easily emit sounds that approximate to fully-formed words – and these from between the lips.

(pause)

Sadly, in some parts of Australia two-thirds of the local population caught trying to form words in articulated sound forms have had four or more placements under Society foster care. Adult fumbling at the runny nose aside, there are over 2,500,0000 children in our community who display the characteristics of fish gobbling for air while stranded in the dumbstruck syndrome. This is an 82% increase in a decade in which the number of muzzle sales declined even after the influx of cheaper Chinese imports sold under the banner of 'Everything under $2'. Clearly, much remains unsung, much remains at throat depth where the bends lurk but not the hand in the pocket. Consequently, one would have to maintain that the current system does not speak well of itself. The lost generations of words have been too long eschewed by the voice boxers in favour of the voice boxees. What chance did our indigenous people have? If we could but stop and listen to the deafening silence of our people's screams, we could understand how on the vast scale of one to ten how many human beings are suffering the agony of being rendered soundless, let alone realise the tremendous strains on the voice boxes of an otherwise small nation. For example, when last was a human presence last heard on the moon? When last has a good word reached the ear of God or any evacuation of wind risen to join the music of the spheres? These are the questions our voice boxes need to be asking.

(voice rising in dramatic effect)

When, in 1948, the brilliant Russian-Jewish vocalist Rachaël ('I Hear You') Lemmings proposed her new concept of "vocicide", she took great care to define it broadly so it meant everything. Vocicide signifies a coordinated plan to destroy any meaningful exchange of sounds within and from within a group of people, including indigenes like our own Australian indigenes, who are not closely tied to slugs and snails and the slitherier like, not meaning our Australian indigenes. Vocicide was defined as reducing words to croaking and then, by both natural and unnatural selection, reducing croaking to corking – commonly known in ENT circles as bunging in the bung. And when the UN Sound Accord followed the Lemmings, whole nations, whole streets suddenly were able to make themselves heard. No longer was the human race going to stand silently by while cultural, political, social, legal, intellectual, spiritual, economic, biological, physiological, psychological, moral, religious and cosmological considerations of the heard-expression type were couched only in nonverbal bugger-yous out of the more elite voice boxes. I mean, come on!

The New Councillor's Augural Speech
(controls herself)

Not only is vocicide, for Lemmings, not confined to mass killing of indigenous peoples -- though it certainly may include their mass suicides in protective mouth-muffs -- it is not necessarily any longer directed at the vicious jibe or the jape at the underbelly of the average voice box, eg, 'how's it hangin'?' and the verbal sucklike.

(pregnant pause)

I have deliberately followed here in the footsteps of Lemmings to illustrate how society once again has the throaty framework, if not the wabbling will, to imagine what sounds-like-human might have sounded like before the critical mass of the silent voice box is reached, if it has not already been reached -- and, I might add, 'speak easy' becomes just another unspoken word or words for a place of eating and drinking illegally.

(pause)

And so, in prohibiting sounds-like-human, the State has unwittingly championed substance dependence on unarticulated noise among even our own Aboriginal groups, like the current wave of car-horn conversations, bumper-against-bumper road rage, etcetera, that are busting to be expressed. No less than one in 20 Australians are now living in households with padded walls, in which no decent voice box has a look-in. Similarly, one in 10 Australians cannot even open his or her mouth for fear of being shushed in the most cruel of manners and for fear of being accused of having a voice box that is non-white. Not even the privacy of toilets has remained sacrosanct for true expression. Everywhere it is no shouting in the library; no putting your verbal foot in at football matches. No voice box these days can be heard enumerating the non-politically correct without first having a short back'n'sides. Those who say with sign-language of the vox box that all this is going too far need only look at the enormous success of Channel 7's 'Look

Who Stays Flabbergasted!'. This is a dumb-down
experience to the disadvantaged a-hem. Not one of our
indigenous people's stolen generations has been returned
during its airing. Not one.

(pause)

With over a quarter of a million notifications of suspected
verbalisations per annum, Australia has the second
highest notification rate in the world... yet only one in
five of these cases comes before a judge. In some
Australian States one in seven citizens can now expect to
be mouth-gagged, subject to a vocal-protection
notification by the time they can say 'up youse for the
rent'. These people must be fed intravenously, but no one
says a word. In Cleveland, Ohio, this has reached the
absurd level of one in two African-American born in
China and one in five Caucasian children born to
Mongoloid parents emerging from the womb with only
vestigial vocal cords. More: huge numbers of dumbstruck
families are "investigated" but too few receive the help
they need. Many parents, mostly low income single
indigenous mothers, are crying out against such
investigations, thus paradoxically increasing the risk of
suppression orders to both themselves and their children.
Our no-child-to-be-heard welfare/sound-insulation
systems are placed under enormous vocal strain, making
them dangerous places for anyone daring to rail against a
system that sticks in the craw like a tuning fork or a stuck
pig on a bull-roarer, especially of the China-manufactured
kind on the most tenuous dangle.

(dramatic pause)

So what can be done? While we do not know how to
prevent all bad people from sneaking silently up on us, a
sound public-health approach which tackles the
underlying risk factors of stunting vibrations from voice
boxes even from Aboriginal Australia holds great
promise. We should sound out the following possibilities:

127

The New Councillor's Augural Speech

1. Address indigenous poverty and poor housing to reduce parental shouting words they regret later and which irrevocably strain voice-box relations at the family and community levels.

2. Strengthen all vibrating muscles of the body, including sphincters and anything around creaky joints, with concrete health services making their voices heard in order to support all new indigenous babies, excluding concrete-floor bouncing exercises under five.

3. Provide free, quality elocution lessons for those with the rudiments of talking and encourage talking to spread to neighbouring tribes where any are left – or where none are left, carry out extensive voice-box evacuations on the full diggy-dog.

4. Resource local communities, regions, nations, space programs to encourage sounds-like human to mimic what we have come to expect from fire and water, wind and sky, and corroborrees where the ground around the central voice box is kept sacred.

5. Improve the knowledge of all professions working with, and teaching of, languages in the form of words, by redefining the shameful and bringing back the outburst, providing no outburst is more than one sound long, that sound to be decided by local tribal committee or with waddies.

6. Enhance the capacity of domestic violence, dementia and drug and alcohol dependence to create greater awareness of beneficial effects of making oneself heard while sniffing the double-sounded word petrol.

7. Replace the word 'adjectives' with 'alcohol' in 'Adjectives and Children Don't Mix' advertising campaigns.

8. Throw out the Outback, although no one knows why.

9. Overthrow all forms of government, from the smallest council to the highest international forum, that have replaced the gravely voices with the gavel. Support the

'Kill the Murderers of Rhyme and Verse or Any Other
Bastard' petition and convince the indigenous population
they started it all.

9. Fart, not to put a too fine a point on it; don't fluff. Give
your voice box full rein. Practise eating with your mouth
open for at least two hours a day. Reward snoring.
Talking in one's sleep should no longer be penalised.

10. Finally, if you're out in the bush or kicking around
Redfern and you come across a lost voice, tread on it and
stop the infection in its tracks.

    (pause for effect)

It is time to go beyond a world where only Nature has its
say. We are in the 21st Century now, and the sooner we
recognise that the human race, regardless of the colour of
the horn pipe, has a right to give voice to its most earnest
voice-box honks. Even tonks, really, if you think about it.
Surely it is time for us all to be reminded that, once upon
a time, there was such a thing as literature... that there
once was a man called Shakespeare who had no fear nor
favour of pronouncing his own name. His voice was not
boxed in! So, let us all aim to let voice boxes once again
bloom right here in Australia! And let us all eschew the
populist cry that too much sticks in the throat here!
Enough! Not a word more! If the stolen generations of
our indigenous people cannot demand to be heard as
really stolen – and not just said to have been stolen – then
what hope is there of any of us clearing our throats?

    (end pause)

Lastly, forgive my throat. It's the frog's fault.

    (She waits defiantly while lighting fades)

(end)

The New Councillor's Augural Speech

Requiem for Anzac Days

(a rank-and-file hymn/short play)

Requiem for Anzac Days

Workshop in classical drama staging.

A rank-and-file requiem. This 'one-acter' is loosely based on the now-discontinued 'Letters from Iraq' web-site and the writing of Edward Nugent, co-author of 'Me, the Old Man'. Traditional airs and voices are used to hopefully weld their World War 1 and Middle East experiences into one free verse hymn-of-lament/hymn-of-praise.

Requiem for Anzac Days

Cast
Cast for five parts as seen necessary

Setting
Suggested to be staged as might a Greek tragedy with darkened area illuminated with spotlit movements

Requiem for Anzac Days

(Darkened stage with areas illuminated by spotlight for the various parts)

CHORUS (strophe):
I not only write books. I am the book. That actual person or persons.

CHORUS (anti-strophe)
Life is. Becoming is. Lie to borne.

ARIA:
In Flanders Fields the poppies blow
Between the crosses, row on row
That mark our place; and in the sky
The larks, still bravely singing, fly
Scarce heard amid the guns below

RECITATIVE 1:
Dear Dad, well, here I am in the land of the Bible. It feels strange. It doesn't seem right. Anyway, this shot shows Greg and Chook and Lofty on the Bushmaster with me. Greg's on the roped-in Browning and Lofty's over by the MAG-58. It's taken at the same place as last week's car bomb, Dad. An Iraqi civvy collared one from a sniper right in the middle of the intersection you see here off to the right. You should have seen Chook; he didn't bat an eyelid but ran out and dragged a woman to safety. He'd fire, drag her, fire again, drag a bit more, fire again. Strange how Chook was all cut up about it after all his time over here. It's his second tour. I'm telling you sometimes it's hard when you're a constant target but

then you also get to start feeling a bit sorry for what they're going through too.
(separating pause)
This is what Captain Robert Nyugen has imparted.

ARIA:
In Flanders Fields the poppies blow
Between the crosses, row on row

RECITATIVE 2:
I married the wrong woman, you were right. I worked my fingers to the bone over that woman before she threw me out and I wound up in hospital. NERVES. The doctor had plenty to say to her, all unpleasant. Anyway I joined the R.N.A.S. while I was over here. They thought I was an Irishman. Don't ask me why, I thought I'll have a go. I was sent to Codfort. In the morning your breath would come out as steam. Cold fish for breakfast and Maconochie stew for dinner. After all this I was sent up to Roehampton where I was taught about sub balloons. After this I was sent to Sheerness and put on a cruiser HMS Mingarry. Supposed to be looking for Subs. Never seen any. This cruiser seemed to want to do to the bottom and stay there. On the move again shortly after that. This time Farnborough. Parachute training. Jump out and hope the thing has been carefully packed. Now that I've been trained it's France. Up I go with camera and then all hell breaks loose. The Jerries throw everything at us and our mob's cursing us to hell for all the disturbance we are causing. I'm not worried about anything but the planes which I know will soon be over with their blasted incendiaries.
(separating pause)
This is what Edward Nugent has imparted.

CHORUS (strophe):

I am the book. I am the person or persons.

CHORUS (anti-strophe)
Unfirmed is. Unfixed is. Is flow.

ARIA:
Between the crosses, row on row
That mark our place; and in the sky

RECITATIVE 1:
… here's a new mate I made said his name was Joe
probably Mohammed like they all say Joe he and his
friends took my last cherry ripes there goes our main diet
out on patrol, ha ha, but who cares when you see Joe's
chocolate lips I thought I'd practise my Arabic on him
with marhaban shismeck meaning I think hello what's
your name and he waves me off with hey mister you got
sister like he's all of ten. If all the Iraqis didn't want to
gut you, Mum, it's surprising how beautiful a lot of their
houses are inside. We did a house search a few weeks
ago before dawn and the whole thing was a bit of a
shambles, kicking in gates bashing down doors the poor
buggers being banged out of their bed thingos. I bashed
on this door and an old codger comes to the door bowing
away sir please come in please sir so I gave him a
chocolate freddo and said go back to sleep Pops.
    (separating pause)
This is what Captain Robert Nyugen has imparted.

RECITATIVE 2:
At last the powers that be decided we had had enough so
we carried on right through Italy to a place named
Taranta. We stopped at different places to use toilet and
get tea and the usual maconochie stew. The man
maconochie must have made a fortune out of this stew.
We got on a boat at Taranta. As soon as I sighted de

137

Requiem for Anzac Days

Lessops statue I knew where we were, Port Said. We
were allowed ashore and there I had my first view of the
Egyptians. They didn't seem to like us very much but
would sell their stuff. All fakes. Turn it upside down and
it was marked, Made in Birmingham. The suffering I have
seen is beyond imagination. France, spotting from kite
balloon behind the lines for artillery, shot down twice,
bailed out, powers in charge decided to send us to Egypt,
was brought back, tunic and all clothing taken off and
steamed. The rest of us thrown in creosote tank to get rid
of lice. Was put on train. Floors covered, carriages were
there for horses and smelt like it. When it rained as it did
once a year it never stopped. I'm thinking and here I am,
only twenty-three.

(separating pause)

This is what Edward Nugent has imparted.

CHORUS (strophe)
I am this book. I am this book. The person or persons.

CHORUS (anti-strophe)
Vision speaks. Words are open hands. Seeing is. Sight
is.

ARIA:
That mark our place; and in the sky
The larks, still bravely singing, fly
Scarce heard amid the guns below

RECITATIVE 1:
Thanks for the snap of Nathan in his soccer getup, Dad.
God willing I'll be seeing him going off the school soon. I
email Franny everyday so don't worry Mum. Now I took
this shot cos at dawn it's mostly I think of you all. It's
like praying I guess. If you look real close can you
imagine the sun coming up and melting the pastels away

138

somehow getting into your waking up pushing back the
rotten brain storms for a bit. Don't worry we've got the
best equipment and we're the troopers. Greg says these
sunsets are the unstruck music of the universe you can
just see the Euphrates it's that mother-of-pearl strip in the
middle of the Promised Land it makes you think about the
bible and how lucky we are back home. But there was a
bombing in a petrol station here and they say the fire was
so intense, mothers were throwing their kids out of the
window to save them from burning alive. Sorry about
getting all maudlin...

(pause)

This is what Captain Robert Nyugen has imparted.

RECITATIVE 2:

The driver of this train seemed as if he never wanted to
get anywhere at this speed. I am a crack shot so I let the
driver have a bullet just above his head. I said I want this
blasted train stopped every 4 hours to enable me to get
some tea. I would run up to the engine and fill my tin up
with water from the boiler. On my return to Kantara the
CO sent for me. I wondered what the hell have I done. It
was nothing. He only asked me if I would accept a
commission. I said no, I just want to get back home. I
made a mistake when I joined up with the British. War.
Syphilis. GONORRHEA. LICE. A Parade. Naked. You
have one of these complaints, Whose fault? YOURS.
You caught it where? The most likely place, Skin St,
Marseilles, France. Anyone picking up a woman there
was asking for trouble. The medical officer lifts up your
penis with a pencil. If you are of these who can't do
without a woman and can pray, start praying.

(pause)

This is what Edward Nugent has imparted.

CHORUS (strophe)

I am this book or books. One pilot had incendiary bullet through both legs. There was a hole beside him in the other pilot.

CHORUS (anti-strophe)
Shadow stopped. Kindled rekindled. Spark is. Starting is keep. Keep is on.

ARIA:
We are the dead. Short days ago
We lived, felt dawn, saw sunset glow,

RECITATIVE 1:
You'll scream with laughter when you hear this one, Mum. When the incoming siren went and they said to evacuate the mess tent no problems there but do you know they all still scrapped their food into the bins and stacked their trays before bolting for cover. Is that great training kicking in or what? Would you believe tomorrow will be my 100th patrol? That's right; time flies when you're having fun, ha ha, but I look at my guys and I think where have you come from am I good enough to watch your backs. It's the most important thing I've ever had to do. I hope I'll never forget it or after all this is over – you know, worry over things that don't matter.
(pause)
This is what Captain Robert Nyugen has imparted.

RECITATIVE 2:
Well, here's Heliopolis, Egypt. Started off with brand new Wellington. Loaded with fuel, Ammo for Malta. Lovely morning. Give pilot course. Got to Malta. They had to shove some Spits out of the way so we could land. Malta was in a hell of a state. Got the stuff off and started for England. Half way, got a radio message from England. Germans playing hell over Channel and south of

England. Another radio message Gatwick fogged up. I
asked how about Biggen hill, No good, fogged up. I
asked the pilot if he had enough fuel. Not a chance. Well
there's only one thing. Hendon. We get to Hendon and
there were planes all over the place. I said to pilot get
higher. No reply so I went to see what was the matter.
One pilot had incendiary bullet through both legs. There
was a hole beside in the other pilot. I took off auto-pilot
and got as high as I could. The Spits seeing the danger
we were in flew around us to give us some protection. I
had to side slip a lot to lose speed. Ground's air gunners
seeing that I could use the plane had gained some
confidence now. The ground staff were excited and I
was getting fed up with their chatter. I said for Christ's
sake shut up I can manage. I picked out a grassy place
and touched down. I didn't do much damage. There was
fire and first aid wagons all over the place but I couldn't
care less. I had saved crew, plane and most important,
myself. Only the good die young, ha ha.

   (pause)
This is what Edward Nugent has imparted.

CHORUS (strophe):
I am the book. I am the planes. I am the sky in the
trenches. The actual person or persons.

CHORUS (anti-strophe):
Dreaming is. Dreaming reaching. Dreaming dawning is.

ARIA:
We lived, felt dawn, saw sunset glow,
Loved and were loved, and now we lie
In Flanders Fields.

RECITATIVE 1:

141

Requiem for Anzac Days
Mum and Dad this shot shows Greg and Chook and Lofty
mad buggers on the LRPV with me are Greg on the FN
Browning M2 and Lofty on the MAG-58 machine gun
this patrol was sort of average five stinking days all over
44C moving east west going south got all the trouble
though from the north town called Hit near the Euphrates
not a sand dune in sight no trees no shade except our
vehicle. The lens don't pick up the mirages or the flies.
You can just see the Euphrates in the background it's the
mother-of-pearl strip in the background. It shines its
water of life they say there's giant water lilies there being
in the middle of the Promised Land, like I said before. It
makes you want to stop and think of the bible and that's
the thing see... us being here at all.
(pause)
This is what Captain Robert Nyugen has imparted.

ARIA:
... and now we lie
In Flanders fields, In Flanders fields
And now we lie in Flanders fields

RECITATIVE 2:
Planes this time. France and Egypt again. I made a great
mistake when I joined up again. I put my war ribbons on
so naturally everyone turned to me as a man of
experience. Instead of marching in fours, everyone was
marching in threes. I had to learn, quickly, so back to
books. Whilst others were out enjoying themselves I was
intent on books on movements, guns etc. Books are
friends. They teach you how to think quickly you are
alert and out think the other fellow.
(pause)
This is what Edward Nugent has imparted.

CHORUS (strophe)
I not only write books. I am the book or books. The actual person or persons.

CHORUS (anti-strophe):
What is what. Sleep was. Final is. Capture is. Release was.

ARIA:
Take up our quarrel with the foe:
To you from failing hands we throw
The torch; be yours to hold it high.
If ye break faith with us who die…

RECITATIVE 1:
Mum and Dad, I really hope this letter never gets to you but if it does tell my darling wife she and our little boy they are the beat of my heart, the soul in my body. They are me without them. I am nothing. If you have to, like, please tell her to bury me then don't grieve too long and move on because I'll still be watching over her and want her and my boy to be happy. I am… I am… it's hard to stop but it's hard to go on, you know? You know, Mum and Dad…?
　　　(pause)
This is what Captain Robert Nyugen has imparted.

RECITATIVE 2:
You take a good look at yourself, get THINKING. You are the sun. an inferno of matter thrown out from the galaxy. I am pieces of this sun split up into planets, one of these the earth first started, life as we know it, I am not only this book but pieces of the Earth that was then in a molten state. Rocks. Everything was molten, Flames upwards and down-wards all over the shop.
　　　(pause)

143

Requiem for Anzac Days
This is what Edward Nugent has imparted.

CHORUS (strophe)
I am not only this book, but piece of this rock. I am
pieces of this sun split up into planets.

CHORUS (anti-strophe)
Many are. One is. Shines many and one. Remembering
is. Name is.

ARIA:
We shall not sleep, where poppies grow
In Flanders fields, in Flanders fields
We shall not sleep, where poppies grow
In Flanders fields, In Flanders fields.

RECITATIVE 1:
Captain Ryan C. Gasser writes: 'Dear Mr and Mrs
Nyugen, Myself and all of the officers who knew your
son wish to express our sincerest sympathy with you in
your great loss. He was killed on 18 July while
courageously trying to defend his wounded men after
their patrol vehicle had been disabled by enemy rocket
fire in the region called Epehy. He was always cheerful
and enthusiastic. He never shirked his duty and never
flinched to face down any danger. Indeed, I have often
heard his men saying they would follow him anywhere.'

RECITATIVE 2:
The afternoon radio slot 'News at 5', 5AN Adelaide
broadcasts: 'This afternoon, the fire brigade was called to
the Eventide men's hostel at Linden Park. Fire fighters
found the charred body of a 79-year-old man in a room
they believed the fire started in...'

144

CHORUS (strophe)
I not only write books. I am the book. That actual person
or persons. The old man has gone devoutly to his Creator.

CHORUS (anti-strophe)
Kept is. Comfort is. Love being. Blooming is. Is bloom.

ARIA:
In Flanders fields the poppies blow
Between the crosses, row on row,
That mark our place; and in the sky
The larks, still bravely singing, fly
Scarce heard amid the guns below.

In Flanders fields, in Flanders fields
We shall not sleep, where poppies grow
In Flanders fields, In Flanders fields.

(Lighting fades)

(end)

Requiem for Anzac Days

The Monkey and the Half-goddess

(a one-act tattle tale)

The Monkey and the Half-goddess

A tattle tale in one act, even sporting a moral.

The pair are brought bound and gagged before the Talls reteller to get them out of their infectious misery before they contaminate the whole community. Of course and as ever always, the troubadour has the perfect shaggy dog for them... that of the tale of the monkey and the half-goddess. As obvious as it might seem, at the core of their miserableness is not just being hitched to each other, nor being New Zealanders, but the mutual dislike for the taste of bananas.

How they are cured of this and brought out of their contagious misery is nothing short of a filthy-bummed thievery on either part, as any once-upon-a-time king could have told them.

Adapted from the author's own book 'The 1001 Lankan Nights' (not 'The 1001 Arabian Nights').

Cast

WI   the Talls reteller here acting a type of marriage
councillor
JANEEN   one half of the married couple
MAX   the other half of the married couple
THE MONKEY
THE HALF-GODDESS
THE KING bit part

Various court servants running around in full liveries and
full circles

Note: With some manipulation, the Monkey and the
Half-goddess can be played by Janeen and Max rising to
assume the roles, and then quickly returning to their initial
'bound-up' places as need be.

The Monkey and the Half-Goddess

(A man and a woman are sitting side-by-side. Apart from being miserable because they are gagged and bound by rope, however loosely, they are miserable in their marriage. This is obvious in their body language towards the close proximity of the other.

Across from them, in a position of any troubadour worth his salt, sits WI, who is contemplating their sadness with a guru's penchant for sympathetic contemplation.

Once WI starts to speak, though, it is hard to stop him…)

WI: Why are you guys so miserable? Others have been born in New Zealand and learnt to smile. Others have been born in New Zealand and got married and learnt to be happy poling their tongues out for tattoos. Even the elephant that delivered you to this appointment had to be reassured that the misery guts you're spilling wasn't the virulent New Zealand kind used by its native African poachers. For the sake of a smile or two, is that fair on an elephant?

(He removes their gags)

JANEEN: (utter surliness) You cured my chafe yet?

The Monkey and the Half-goddess
WI: I don't know. Have I?

MAX: (equally sour) Dumber than he looks, you believe?

JANEEN: Useless.

MAX: A real drong.

WI: You have come with a note that says, 'Beware; they bring misery as instant freeze'. Oh dear, don't you realise that, first, there is a sky of brilliant white cloud bloom so brilling, bright and calm with the fleckers to come?

JANEEN: What's he on about, mopoke?

MAX: What's he on about, droopy?

WI: Have both of you forgotten, just because you could never have heard, of the king in his fine flummery back in his frenchy-fine old palace sliced around the other side of the sun to where you anywhere are? No? Good God! God Gob! Goob Goddle! No wonder they sent you to me. Well...

(He pause for dramatic 'once-upon-a-time' effect)

JANEEN: Did that there king have a chafe?

MAX: Did he have to keep listening to her chafe?

WI: What the king did have was this peculiarity. As the Talls retellings go, it was a once-upon-a-time palace and the storybook king of all this lived there most of the time, as who-wouldn't? But when this once-upon-a-time king wasn't in his once-upon-a-time palace, he disguised those ten-acre grounds as a fourteen-hectare grounds and the

152

splendid palace itself as an ordinary sort of house in order to discourage thieves which of course encouraged thieves. (pause)

So, this time, in the now of the retelling, as he did not so very often, the king came out of lapidary where he was counting his precious stones to sew on for the once-upon-a-year carnival of his summer dresses where he could show his people his right royal dress sense. There were so many different prints and colours and styles, he didn't know where to start apart from starting from his bottom up. Picture that!

(A spot on the KING in front of a mirror and dragging up)

WI: What a queen and so gay! What a wardrobe and wimple! He paraded those summer dresses throughout the length and breadth of his land's shopping malls with handbags on the hooks and tickets on the hangers-on and the breathless on the speechless; and he did it also down streets paved and duck-boarded, up and down town, over'n'above open sewers in a burst of gay parade and parody. It was all his once-upon-a-year time, yes, of showing off his summer dresses so that his people knew what they were fighting the hard graft of life to keep him in dresses for.

(and)

Meanwhile, as I said, the palace turned into a house was not without its thieves and each year never was.

(He starts off with suspense whisper, while the KING disappears to be replaced on one side and the other by the MONKEY and the HALF-GODDESS enacting:)

153

The Monkey and the Half-goddess
WI: Upstairs, the monkey was quietly shaking one
window pane loose, reaching out from the end of a bough.
And meanwhile along the same sort of lines, downstairs,
the half-Goddess was twisting a few hinges loose with her
fingernails, but covered with gloves so she wouldn't leave
any fingerprints that might show up next year somewhere
on the king's summer prints. You can see how it goes...

(They watch the MONKEY and the HALF-
GODDESS for a necessary time, and:)

WI: And thus it was that each year, unbeknown to each
other, the monkey and the half-goddess did this on the
same day at the same time and the same glum faces full of
misery.
   (pause)
It was not to say she was ugly; it was not to say the
monkey was not ugly; they just looked alike and it just
looked a bit crook. In fact, they were, both, not the
cleanest of thieves to set before a king. They both had
things about their private parts which might explain why
they were loners, each. The monkey had been rolling
around in 3B best-drawing graphite somewhere turning
his anal display into a bit of a leaden dud and his bare
breasts duddier than the usual dud monkey-lovers would
be used to. The half-goddess had the imprints of the
poverty of owning only one dress and with the
consequence of 3B best-drawing graphite-type hand
smudges where bikini cloth would be if she was part of
the king's beach fashion parade which she wasn't because
he kept all bikinis to model himself so that the really-wide
welter of his eating wasn't shown by contrast or by half.
Besides, these great bikini smears on the half-goddess's
private parts were from her rucking up her panties and
hoisting up her bras a lot more than she perhaps ought to,
but nobody dared to ask why. They looked chafey, did the
154

monkey and the half-goddess. They weren't the most pleasant respective monkey and half-goddess the world had seen.

(As the MONKEY and the HALF-GODDESS enter the palace at top and below:)

WI: Having broken into the top floor of the house, the monkey would eat all it could find up there except any banana which it hated, and would rip apart everything it could lay its claws on. It particularly delighted in leaving a stool on the king's bed as its calling card. Also, from the window, it made sure it threw rocks at anybody passing down below or even minding their own businesses strolling along past the king's pad pretending to be a house. When it couldn't make any more people more miserable, it would start throwing stones down the staircase at whoever it heard each and every year moving around downstairs and stopping it from having the whole place to itself. Year after year, always, yes, the same once-upon-a-time.

(and the same:)

The half-goddess, despite her name, was not much better than the monkey. Once inside downstairs, she would guts down all she could eat except any banana which she thought was bad for her chafe, would tear up everything she could get her claws into, loved leaving a stool in the king's bathroom's wash basin as a calling card. She too made sure she threw rocks and break as many heads of the passers-by as she could and give the people minding their own businesses passing the king's pad the... pardon my king's English... shits. Then, too, when she couldn't make any more people any more miserable, she would throw rocks up the stairs at whoever it was she heard up there every year stopping her from having the whole place to herself.

155

The Monkey and the Half-goddess

*(They let all this play out before their imaginaries.
WI resumes when the MONKEY and the HALF-
GODDESS have 'caught up'. When they have, the
king's chef and servants take over and bustle
around with:)*

WI: As silly as it looked, the king wasn't as silly as the
cuts of some of his summer dresses. He was quite aware
that each year at summer-dress parade time the monkey
broke into his palace pretend house and ransacked only
upstairs because it was scared of the somebody it heard
downstairs.
    (and)
Likewise, the king knew the half-goddess every year
broke in downstairs and only ransacked down there
because she was wary of whoever it was she heard
moving around upstairs. Also, every year the only things
left untouched either by the monkey upstairs or the half-
goddess downstairs were the bananas. So he ordered all
the food taken out of the house save for one banana to be
disguised as a banquet not only fit for a king but also for
modern-day thieves with their penchant for the higher
things of life than kings, especially when it came to
summer dresses and bananas and monkey and half-
goddesses -- and he ordered that it, the banana disguised
as a king's banquet, should be placed on the staircase
exactly between them, exactly half on the monkey's side
of upstairs and exactly half on half-goddess's side of
downstairs.

    *(allows the king's servants to catch up and remove
    themselves all very blusterly)*

WI: Well! Well may you sit there with your mouths
wide open! It straightaway happened like that too, as

these things retold tend to do as tall tales that tattle. Both the monkey and the half-goddess tried to creep up or down the stairs to get to the banquet left midway there as the only food they could steal that was at all fit for a monkey better than a king and a half-goddess better than a king. Looking down at the banquet the monkey thought the spread looked a king's banquet just made for it...

MONKEY: That looks a king's banquet just made for me.

WI: ...and looking up at the banana-as-king's-banquet the half-goddess thought the spread looked just about made for her and her chafe.

HALF-GODDESS: Well, I say that king's banquet looks just made for me and my chafe.

WI: They could creep down the stairs, could creep up the stairs. They could stretch their arms out as far as they could and nearly get to touch that banquet. But each time they got near to it, they were pushed back by hearing whoever it was up there and whoever it was down there sneaking around like some thief in the night copying what they were trying to do.
(pauses to watch them)
Not that they gave up trying. Each was so sick of being pushed around year after once-upon-a-year by whomever it was always stopping them from having the whole place to themselves that each hid on the landing above and below the banquet left for them and waited for nightfall.

(Long breathless pause as best possible)

WI: At midnight, of course, no moonlight of course, each made a dash for the fit-for-a-king's-banquet that was

157

really only a banana and, of course, they collided front on right on half way. The monkey and the half-goddess thought:

MONKEY: What a filthy black smudge of a human being; I can do her, no worries.

HALF-GODDESS: What a filthy black bum of a monkey; I can do it, no worries.

WI: With that, they fought. Oh, didn't they ever!

(They do so. Over the action:)

WI: They fought so hard they wound up in adjacent beds at the local hospital that normally was the king's karaoke bar whether it was the king's summer-dress season or not. This was too much. The monkey closed it eyes; and kept them closed for shame.

MONKEY: No way am I going to be seen here lying in this hospital next to someone who looks like a thieving-arsed half-goddess any monkey would be ashamed to be seen with.

WI: Likewise, the half-goddess closed her eyes against that hospital reality, and kept them closed for shame, going:

HALF-GODDESS: No way am I going to be seen here in this hospital next to something that looks like a thieving-arsed monkey no half-goddess would want to be seen anywhere near.

WI: Instead, they pretended they were back in the king's pretend house licking their wounds on the staircase on either side of the king's banquet left fit for them. The trouble was each of them was thinking with a mixture of miserable sullenness and miserable cunning, not a good combination on empty stomachs not lined with any binding banana fibre.

MONKEY: (miserably) How am I, the most decent monkey I know, going to get my head around being prevented from getting to that king's banquet anyone can see was set out for me by this thieving-arsed filthy thing shuffling around in the dark making like a snooty half-goddess all chafed-up?

WI: Not that the half-goddess wasn't thinking the same...

HALF-GODDESS: How am I, the most decent half-goddess I know, going to get my head around being prevented from getting to this king's banquet anyone can see was fit for me by this thieving-arsed filthy thing shuffling around in the dark making like a snooty monkey all chafed-up?

MONKEY: Why should I be run off by a half-goddess with a tail between her legs when I'm cleverer?

HALF-GODDESS: Why should I be run off by a monkey with a tail between its legs when I'm cleverer?

(a blackout as quick as a wink)

WI: But when it opened its eyes the monkey was sitting half in the stool the half-Goddess had left in the king's bathroom wash basin downstairs and half not sitting in it.

MONKEY: (confused, outraged) Hey...!

159

The Monkey and the Half-goddess

WI: (urgency) The monkey's first reaction finding itself down there in the poo was to panic before it realised it had better disguise itself as the half-goddess quick smart so that if she caught him down there she'd only confuse herself.

(The MONKEY changes costume elements)

WI: Likewise, when the half-goddess opened her eyes and found herself in the poo upstairs, half sitting pretty much in the stool the monkey always left in the middle of the king's bed and half not sitting in it…

HALF-GODDESS: (ditto confused, outraged) Hey…!

WI: …that she got so scared of being taken off by the monkey into the jungle as one of its own and losing her virginity before she ever found it again after hanging it out to dry somewhere one time. So she quickly disguised herself as a chimp so if that thieving filthy-arsed monkey caught her it would only confuse itself.

(The HALF-GODDESS affects her monkey disguise)

WI: So, there you are. In their new disguises upstairs and downstairs there, neither dared move, despite where they had found themselves half-sitting which was really in the do-do's. Their faces became as long as some of the king's summer dresses. The king and the entire king's cortege in their summer corsages could return anytime and then they would really be in the poop and not halfway in the shit as they were. Their stomachs were started to rumble with the time they were waiting breathlessly, not to mention thinking it wasn't fair they should be held up

160

like this by a mere monkey or a mere half-goddess not ever a full goddess. You wouldn't see or hear such miserableness!

MONKEY: This ain't fair. She's not even a full goddess.

HALF-GODDESS: This ain't fair. He's only a monkey.

WI: The trouble was neither knew enough magic to know how they had gotten downstairs when they should have been upstairs and upstairs where they should have been downstairs. Yet somehow the half-goddess and the monkey did know this pretty simultaneously:

HALF-GODDESS: I bet it's half-parked in my precious stool. Cheeky. And I bet it's trying to disguise its thieving filthy-arsed half-self as me because it's scared of me. What a cheek!

MONKEY: I bet she's half-parked in my precious stool. Cheeky. And I bet she's trying to disguise her thieving filthy-arsed half-self as me because she's scared of me. What a cheek!

WI: But, you see, they couldn't really help themselves. The half-goddess was going on to think:

HALF-GODDESS: I have to admit, looking down on it, that monkey does look a bit like me.

WI: And the monkey was going on to think:

MONKEY: I have to admit, looking up at here, that half-goddess does look a bit like me.

161

The Monkey and the Half-goddess

WI: In fact the longer they sat in each other's stool looking up and down at the other, the more each started having funny feelings for their lesser halves half-sitting in a stool down there in the wash basin really in the stinko or half-sitting really in the stinko up there on the king's bed.

(pause)

But this is a tattle tale of the tall retelling and we all just know there will be larger appetites in play here, don't we? Hmm? Shall we nod?

(waits until the couple reluctantly nod their heads)

WI: Well, that same night -- and again it would have to be midnight of course in the Talls retelling of it, but this time a full moon of course according to how the clouds get propped up by centuries of narrative around centuries of campfires -- the monkey disguised as the half-goddess crept up the stairs towards the banana-as-king's-banquet at the same once-upon-a-time as the half-goddess disguised as the monkey was creeping down the stairs towards the banana-as-a-king's-banquet. Again they met exactly in the middle of the palace-turned-into-a-house on that stairway there. They stopped in their tracks, not believing what they were seeing, too shocked to move.

(He waits for the re-enactment to catch up)

WI: Now the monkey had to contend with another live monkey. Now the half-goddess had to contend with another live half-goddess. This was too much by half!

HALF-GODDESS: This is too much by half!

MONKEY: This is too much by half!

162

HALF-GODDESS and MONKEY: (together angry/miserable) It is one thing to have to share a palace-cum-house with a half-goddess, up herself, if you were a monkey or to share a palace-cum-house with a monkey, up itself, if you were a half-goddess, but quite another thing to have to share it with another thieving filthy-arsed monkey or another thieving filthy-arsed half-goddess with 3B best-drawing graphite smudged all over their unmentionable parts!

WI: Oh, and didn't they go at each other!

(orchestrating the action:)

WI: They threw themselves. They flung themselves. They went toe-to-toe over that banana-as-king's-banquet. Or they thought they did, thought they were. But this time, there was the moment's hesitation of monkey upon monkey and the moment's hesitation of half-goddess upon half-goddess. And instead of falling upon each other in a crook old way, they found themselves falling into the crooks of each other's arms, going as to confuse even themselves, so look-alike were they anyway:

HALF-GODDESS: Brother!

MONKEY: Sister!

HALF-GODDESS: Sister!

MONKEY: Brother!

HALF-GODDESS: Lover!

MONKEY: Lover!

The Monkey and the Half-goddess

WI: (triumphantly over) If that wasn't enough, the monkey couldn't believe it was hearing itself meaning the banana-as-king's-banquet there, going:

MONEKY: You first.

WI: And the half-goddess couldn't believe she was saying to it concerning the banana-as-king's-banquet there, going:

HALF-GODDESS: No, you first.

WI: So polite, it could have been making each feel really miserable but, strangely, it wasn't. And, the Talls retelling fact of it was: no sooner said than the monkey was buffing off the greasy 3B best-drawing graphite smudges from the half-goddess's private parts and, likewise tiddle-the-do, the half-goddess was buffing off the 3B best-drawing graphite stains from the monkey's private-display-y parts. It was all very familiar, intimate-wise, and full of non-miserable smiles.

(waits while they nit and pick at each other)

WI: And, when they had cleaned each other up, their hearts now on the other's sleeve (out of the king's autumn-wear wardrobe), they sat down to eat together. A fact! They then, in their new-found togetherness, picked ever so primly and ever so simultaneously at the edges of the banana-as-king's-banquet there moving you-first-no-you-first towards the centre which was really only all banana anyway. See, how they did so with such solemn concentration that it really looked like they believed there was something king's-banquetty there other than a banana which each – the half-goddess and the monkey – previously detested the taste of.

164

(turns coquettish, appropriately)
And when there, at the king's-banquet centre of it all,
when their fingers touched -- light in touch, tipple to
tipple, tripped by the tripping up -- it was not lost on the
monkey and it was not lost on the half-goddess as to how,
after all those thieving filthy-arsed years, they had arrived
at the banana at the centre of it'n'them both.

HALF-GODDESS: Goodness, I have arrived at the
banana centre of it all after all these filthy-arsed thieving
years...!

MONKEY: Shit-a-brick, I have arrived at the banana
centre of it all after all these filthy-arsed thieving years...!

WI; (ecstatic) For banana skin was all that was left of the
banana-fit-for-a-king's-banquet there! Not a misery guts
was to be seen! The monkey hadn't even noticed it had
eaten the hated banana. The half-goddess hadn't even
noticed she had eaten the hated banana. In their
realisation of their feelings for each other all along, that
banana that had stood between them had gone poof!

MONKEY: Poof!, would you believe.

HALF-GODDESS: Poof!, it's hard to believe.

*(Climacteric pause. He delivers the lesson-to-be-
learnt)*

WI: Did it discern them, concern them, unlearn them?
The monkey would have thought so. The half-goddess
would have thought so. The king with his all-seeing eye
would have thought so to teach them a lesson about
thieving 3B-graphite anal regions. But they were not

discerned, concerned; they were not unlearned. They
might still say:

MONKEY: I hate bananas.

HALF-GODDESS: I can't stand the thought of the
things, m'self.

WI: But the half-goddess still had to scratch her chafe,
yes. And the thing was they each knew the other was
lying because they had seen otherwise with their own
eyes. No greater love has someone who can trust their
love to be lying! Don't you see that? The king did.

JANEEN: What was the upshot?

MAX: Who cares?

JANEEN: (amazingly lovingly) I do.

MAX: (ditto) I didn't say I didn't.

> *(They throw off the rope that has been involuntarily*
> *binding them and move close, put their arms around*
> *each other.*
>
> *WI nods his vast approval)*

WI: The upshot was a lay-down misere: the monkey
realised it wouldn't be anywhere near the same lonely
miserable sod...

MAX: (taking it personally) Fair go. New leaf.

WI: ...if it just simply disguised itself as the half-goddess
and fed off her similar miserable dislike for bananas. It

was the same for the half-goddess too, of course. She saw how she wouldn't be the same lonely miserable sod-dess…

JANEEN: (taking it just as personally) Hey, don't come the scratch. New leaf here too.

MAX: (cow-eyed at her) Aw.

JANEEN: (ditto at him) Aw, you too.

WI: (carrying on) …if she just disguised herself as the monkey and fed off his similar miserable dislike of bananas. And each of them suddenly saw how all they had to do to be happy was to interchange roles, stay disguised as the other and, at every moment of every day, feed off each other keeping bananas out of the picture.

JANEEN: Dead easy.

MAX: You bet.

WI: There you go. So, in the thereafter of any retellings you can name, when the monkey dressed as the half-goddess, and the half-goddess dressed as the monkey, but still kept their individual thieving 3B-pencil-leaded arses in gear with each other, the king's summer dresses stayed pretty much the same-old, same-old. And the summer seasons rolled on. The monkey even changed over to being the half-goddess's left-handedness; the half-goddess even changed over to being the monkey's right-handedness. She grew its beard; it grew just her hint of a moustache but kept it discreetly waxed. They both displayed their tail-ends a lot, especially as they mooned them out of the windows at the people minding their own business just trying to stroll by their king's pad of a palace on a lazy Sunday afternoon. At least they stopped throwing the rocks down at them.

(All gather for the grand finale)

WI: Don't think any tattle tale of the Talls retelling does not have a purpose. In his foresight with his glasses on and his wisdom with them off, even the king in his summer dresses had foreseen it all. He had left them an escape route -- an exit doorway halfway up the stairs and halfway down the stairs, exactly midway. All they had to do was take the moral of their story, go through the doorway made of lollipops, slide down the barber-pole sugar-candy ladder and feel free to glee away out into the sugar-candy world where chafes were no more. But, much to the king's chagrin, the monkey and the half-goddess didn't take that exit he so kingly offered however much they couldn't stop smiling now.
    (and)
Nature not nurture, you see. They might be happy at last and found true love at last, but the monkey and the half-goddess were still from New Zealand. Meaning that they were still too much of miserable b's deep down to leave any palace they were welcome in, especially when none of the king's guards knew who was who, who was the female and who was the fiery-arsed to sink their boots into... not when they had dug their NZ toes in and had their naked butts sticking out of the window.
    (and)
Nobody was going to tell them to bugger off from anywhere. A sheepsland as that was is where you come out pasteurised and never forget it. And so the monkey and the half-goddess stay and drove the poor king quite mad... mad enough to give up his summer dresses until the next summer and the realm's malls called.

(JANEEN and MAX get up.

She undresses him and puts on his clothes.

At the same time, he undresses her and puts on her clothes.)

JANEEN: Whenever you feel banana-y, feel free to feed off me.

MAX: Whenever you feel a banana coming on, you feel free to feed off me.

JANEEN: Just watch the chafe.

MAX: Where is the chafe?

JANEEN: I don't know. Have you got it?

MAX: Have you?

JANEEN: Bugger the chafe.

MAX: Too right.

JANEEN: (cooing) How it hanging with my mmm-loverly Max?

MAX: Hey, ain't I or aren't I your Janeen?
(coos to her coyness)
And how it's hanging with my lovie Janeen-ny?

JANEEN: Hey, ain't I or ain't I your little Maxie?

(They cuddle, take hands and go lovingly out.

WI waves them goodbye)

WI: (after them) About the chafe, the elephant will be so pleased.

(end)

The Poisoning of Old Messy

(a one-act play)

The Poisoning of Old Messy

A one-act play.

There is a line which no psychiatrist or hypnotist will dare cross

When the geriatric priest is sent by the court to the psychiatrist for sentence evaluation, the line is crossed.

Cast
KISSANE the psychiatrist
FATHER LEW, priest
FATHER GEOFFREY MASSEY 'Old Messy'; retired
priest

Setting
First setting is in a confessional room in a Catholic
church. This has little to do with the traditional
confessional booth but is merely a couple of chairs side-
by-side. At least it is in a separate room with curtains.

Second setting is in a hypnotist's office... again basic
lounging chair and table; nothing much else is needed.

The Poisoning of Old Messy

1.

(In the modern-day confessional room)

KISSANE: Father, excusee, but am I in Confession?

FATHER LEW: Pardon?

KISSANE: And do you still throw back a 'Yes-or-no, my son'? Are we still your sons? Were we ever your daughters? Do you still call it forgiveness of sins? Questions sort of like that.

FATHER LEW: It is the rite of reconciliation, Mr…?

KISSANE: Call me doctor or call me beyond the pail. Kissane's the name; blame's the game. I'm here to consider large-ish questions before God, Father Lew, in a just-asking kind of confessional sort of way.

FATHER LEW: Do you happen to be Catholic?

KISSANE: I came here thinking my questions could be rolled into one, I think. This basically is: do you let your, y'know, new rites of reconciliation get in the way of a good murder?

FATHER LEW: A what?

KISSANE: Murder. Cold-blooded. Pre-meditated, pre-medicated. That kind. Confidentiality-wise by way of reconciliation, of course.

FATHER LEW: Are you making fun?

KISSANE: Forgive me, Father. I said 'Forgive me, Father' at the start. But I was thinking big shame if your new rites of whatever have given confidentiality the boot, though. Confidentiality was big in my days. I know it was big in your day. You were real big on it, I hear tell. Quite right, too. The thing is I currently have these two patients the courts have foisted on me, you know, for judicial psychiatric assessment. You do have a spare moment, don't you, Father?

FATHER LEW: Sorry, I actually don't.

KISSANE: Of course you do. The first one is hairy, real body-hairy, misguided youth type. Scatterbrained will figure in my summary to the court, if and when asked. He's facing the lock-up for dangerous driving without a license; serious stuff. No sooner he's stolen this car from a garage than its front wheel falls off. Right off. Does the real loser stop? Of course not. Like, he's on three wheels, burning up Oakleigh Central, sparks flying everywhere like hell's broken loose, only going faster and faster. He does over three red lights, wipes out the front of a deli, smashes into the chasing cop's car trying to do a U-ie across the Prince's Highway. I have him on my couch and I have to ask why. 'Just to see'. That was his answer. 'Just to see'. Of course none of this really happened to him, but it's a good metaphor for what happened to him in life, see. It gets you thinking, doesn't it? Is this kid really different from any of us as much as the wheel falling off and yet bashing our way faster and

176

faster into greater chaos? I mean, metaphysics over metaphors here, Father.

FATHER LEW: (now worried) Do I need to call for help?

KISSANE: Just a story about the first guy, that's all, Father. The second guy the courts sent me, he's probably more up your alley. This bloke's none other than the very-reverend, very-bloody-fallen Father Geoffrey Massey... you'd remember him, no?

FATHER LEW: (archly) I don't think so.

KISSANE: Keep your nose out of the nasty ordinary rags and in the Catholic Times, do you? The Very Reverend Father Geoffrey Massey O.F.M., ex-dean of Xavier College, hauled out from the pasture for buggering likely lads in the old dorm days of the Seventies? Course he rings a bell. Now, see, Father, I had my first session with old Messy Massey yesterday, court appointed and all that, and your name came up, that's all.
   (to the priest's attempt to rise)
Will you sit the fuck down?!   Sorry, sorry. Five minutes, Father.

FATHER LEW: No.

KISSANE: No what?

FATHER LEW: No, I won't sit the fuck down.

KISSANE: Yes the fuck you will.

   *(It's not a threat, yet the force of his presence
   makes the priest remain where he is)*

177

The Poisoning of Old Messy

KISSANE: At the same time, Father, I have all these other fulltime paying clients but my first guy I mentioned… big spondoolics in the family… maybe, just maybe, he could benefit from joining the alleged victims of old Messy Massey in the case. That's just my opinion. What do you think?

FATHER LEW: What do I think, what?

KISSANE: About this lotsa-clout client of mine, that first real car-wreck of a guy. Should I have him join in on the case? On the one hand his lower lip quivers on how he hates this slur on his dear old Xavier. On the other hand, he's a mess whenever we discuss how he was one who old Messy kept abusing him in the old annexe of the footy pavilion. No metaphor about it. So, will it give him closure or not, Father? No? Yes? Don't care? Pity, because he often mentions you as junior college priest in those days.

FATHER LEW: (growing alarm) No.

KISSANE: You weren't?

FATHER LEW: Maybe.

KISSANE: 'Maybe?' Fibbies here in the confessional?

FATHER LEW: I don't talk about those things.

KISSANE: See, I thought I'd better pop around and get your opinion before I add this first guy's name to the list of accusers of the second guy, Old Messy.

FATHER LEW: I had nothing to do with Father Massey's days… what he did or might have done.

KISSANE: What he says, too, Father.
   (then)
Say, do you happen to remember there was a massage
table or something in the old annexe of the footy pavilion
and old Messy-Massey always doubling as the footy
team's first-aid johnny? Cunning old rooster. Is it true
they named him old Messy because he thought it was a
demo of genteel-ity hawking his gorbies into his white
handkerchief and folding it up and putting it in his
pocket? My poor first guy with the spare dough babbles
on about that there massage table and eucalyptus oil and
how he couldn't wash the smell off, so afterwards he'd be
raked with guilt about his mates guessing his dirty little
secret. He said come and ask you about that.

FATHER LEW: That what?

KISSANE: His dirty little secret. Dirty little secrets,
plural, really. Lots and lots of them. But not the boys.
Apparently, he means about you and bloody old Messy.

   *(FATHER LEW gets up to leave, but is
   overpowered by the force of:)*

KISSANE: Where do you think you're going?!

FATHER LEW: Where do you think you are?

KISSANE: Oh, I forgot. It's a church. Mustn't raise the
old voice in the church. Sorry, sorry. Get involved. My
weak spot as a shrink. Always have. Terrible habit, bad
as needing a snort now and again.
   (sits and becomes quite affable)
Why should I get involved all the time? I mean, half the
time they don't even bother to pay me, the court doesn't.

No, see, Father Lew, I especially wanted to know what you think I ought to do about some poor sod breaking down on my couch and crying out… just let me see my notes here…

(reads from a pad)

'You might think he was only bashing my bum, but what he was really doing was buggering up my mind!'

(and)

Bit lurid, bit dramatic, but you get the picture.

FATHER LEW: No, no!

KISSANE: Oh well, better out than in, I guess. Now, yesterday I had my first court appointment with the old Messy himself. It's always a bit of a bun fight, the first of these court sessions, but I've got to say he certainly didn't look like he'd been yanked out from under a lap blankie to be the biggest sodomite baddie we've had in years, and that's saying something, right?

(forces that)

Right?!

FATHER LEW: How do I know?

KISSANE: (going on) Sure, he was old, Father Brown, ha ha. Old. He was ancient callow-to-colourless. He was an overboiled egg, outdone. There were these sinews down his neck that got me thinking of a dried bat's wing. But remorse, devastation? I might be wrong, Father Lew, but out of that hessian bag of a skull I got only disdain. It was only the first session, of course, but I'll add another 'd'. Defiance. Here's another. He fronted up poofily carrying a single d…d…dahlia. No kidding. He's actually gone all camp pansy on us. What an old fart! You make up your own mind from the tape.

180

FATHER LEW: Tape?

KISSANE: I'm a psychiatrist, Father. There's always a tape.

FATHER LEW: You can keep it.

KISSANE: Oh, I don't want to keep it. I want to give it to you.

FATHER LEW: Leave it at the secretary's office.

KISSANE: (ignoring that) The tape I'm leaving you... the crux, as in crucifix I guess... is when I asked him did he seriously think he could go on for years diddling boys so openly. Yesth, he said, full-on listhpy, because God always forgave him. You'll hear me go the big huh-say-again? to that. God always forgave him, he comes back, because Father Lew never refused him confession afterwards. That's what he said. Father Lew never refused him confession afterwards. Father Lew always got God to forgive him. Father Lew never let him down. Father Lew was always on the side of God. That right, Father Lew?

FATHER LEW: You can't say that.

KISSANE: (sarcastic) You never failed him. Good for you.

FATHER LEW: He was my senior priest!

KISSANE: Hey, steady on. No problemo with me. You ask my first-guy client how persuasive old Messy could be back then. And we get proud of things, I suppose. Common nature. You could be forgiven yourself if you thought you were the deadeye dick of absolutions straight from heaven's gate back then, right? Young and all evangelistic enthusiastic. God shooting from the hip then for you, was it?

(KISSANE has now moved over to block the door. He is obviously not intending to move)

KISSANE: Hey, I'm just saying. What do I know? I was just wondering, though, say how many times might you have given him the big cross and then watched him walking out the door mentally unzipping the next kid he was sniffing down? How many times, give or take?

FATHER LEW: We have rules that I'm not at liberty to discuss.

KISSANE: Certainly not in the confessional.

FATHER LEW: (nodding at logic) Certainly not in the confessional.

KISSANE: I know, I know. By the way, my first-guy client asked me to ask if you remembered him. A skinny little kid he was. Said he was well-known for it. Skinny compounded by a skull-crust crew-cut. A bit of a goer at footy. Seventy-eight? Don't remember him? They even called him Skinny. Seems nobody can remember him anymore. Poor guy of a car wreck, it seems it really gets to him, that. But then that's why he's a nutcase, tilting at windmills, ha ha, right?
   (and)
But, to my mind, he has a good point about the confessions, though. Did you keep them up because they made you feel, you know, you were in the know? That you were in the daisy chain between God and Old Messy?

Did you think God Himself put you in that daisy chain?
Didn't they have any Archbishops and police back then?
No? No reaction?

*(FATHER LEW makes a real effort to get past him
to leave)*

KISSANE: If you leave the tape goes in without you
hearing it!

FATHER LEW: The Church won't be threatened.

KISSANE: Beg to differ there, Father. Doesn't seem the
Church is too hot-the-trot on going overboard for its
rampant diddlers these days. Not like around '78 and
assistant priest days; I get it.
    (and)
I get back to how I started... if you did nothing about Old
Messy then, how are you going to do anything about
coldblooded murder now?

FATHER LEW: What murder?

KISSANE: Thought you'd never ask, Father. I brought
you a few pressies, Father. This one's a tape of
yesterday's session with old Messy plus a few of my own
first-guy's observations about all that. And here's my
card with tomorrow's appointment for old Messy just in
case you'll want to know where he'll be and where I'll be
and where you should be.

(He thrusts these into the priest's hands)

KISSANE: If I were you, I'd get there early so you can
watch him walk in. You won't often get a chance to see

183

how your yesterday's absolution begets his today's
mincing sashay.

(He is obviously going to leave himself. The priest can
regain his dignity)

FATHER LEW: Can I go now?

KISSANE: (hard) No.

　　　(FATHER LEW is taken aback)

KISSANE: Why don't you just sit there? After all,
you're so good at confessionals.

FATHER LEW: I'm leaving.

KISSANE: (threat again) I don't think so.

FATHER LEW: I'm leaving.

KISSANE: Sit there and listen to the tape, then you're
leaving.

FATHER LEW: You said you were going to sin.

KISSANE: I am. I will be. Just being here… inviting
you to come tomorrow… is against the law of the court.
And stuff you for it, Father Lew.

　　　*(He is physically overbearing as he moves and
　　　switches on the tape.*

　　　Blackout.

　　　During the blackout:)

184

TAPE OVER: Recording Wednesday 8 April. Copy for
Father Lew tomorrow. Subject: Massey evaluation. Plus
my verbal reading of notes given to me by client known
here as Skinny (Jane: cross reference for office copy,
okay?) and included on his, Skinny's, own insistence.
    (pause)
Father Lew, first a little preamble by me before you hear
Skinny's thoughts or the Old Messy session. I'm going to
briefly describe my office to you because I've just
realised I'm going to invite you here for tomorrow's
session. Usual thing overlooking St Kilda Road, the
marches of the autumn-beaten elms outside. Quite lovely,
really. Inside here, I've always quite liked the smell of
real leather as evidence I'm capable of a little
competence. Even a couch. Some of us still have 'em,
you'll be glad to know.
    (and)
So, next you'll hear me reading Skinny's notes on today's
Old Messy's session. When you come tomorrow I'll tell
you about him... that's Skinny... perhaps. I had given
him permission to be sitting in my waiting room when
they brought Old Messy in today. I took precautions
against any possible confrontation, although whether my
decision will have any impact on the cold-blooded murder
thing I'm probably going to mention to you, I don't know.
Anyhow. Skinny actually wanted you to hear his thoughts
on seeing the old boy after so many years. I'm a terrible
reader, but here we go anyway... and I'm reading
Skinny's notes here:
    (notes read)
'Doctor Kissane, I actually had to stop myself from
jumping up and hiding. The old bastard didn't even look
like he was under arrest. The same old sneer; the same
old barging through with that infuriating conceit. He's
still so lean and cruel-looking! It was almost as if my

185

images of predators have always actually been what I was
imprinted by him. Until they closed the door of your
office on him, there was no way I... the slightest little
movement I couldn't do, you know? I could actually feel I
couldn't move a muscle if I tried. I felt fixed in
headlights. Don't ask me why. I have no idea. There he
was... pathetic. It wasn't nerves -- or not all nerves -- but
something else. You said ghosts. Alright, ghosts.

(and)

'If I was in there now with him and doing that assessment
thing on him instead of you... oh, sure, I'd be trying to
crucify him with guilt and all that, but I just know it'd be
a sham... that somehow, maybe, I should be sitting where
he is. It's not nerves, no. I think it's something far worse.
I was quivering with anticipation. He came, walk passed
me... walked, like, through me... and I'm feeling the
same thing, some constant thing at last about him.

(and)

It feels like it's the same filthy thrill I used to have back
then when he was abusing me. God help me, I'm not
kidding. The nearer he must have been getting to your
door, the more I was back on that massage table with the
hot heat of that eucalypt oil sucking me up still, waiting
for him to come in and bolt that old wooden door again,
smiling that sick-making way, and those bastard wet lips
of his, licking away.

(has to gather himself)

I did, I felt that rough old towel draped over my cock
again. His susshing sounds of secret, secrets. The thing
made thrilling, again and again. The worse thing is and
was: he knew me. He understood me. How can that be?

(pause)

That's the thing, see, Dr Kissane. Who's the worst when
it gets boiled down? Godalmighty, maybe he was only
the giver and I the wanter.

(and)

The dirty fucking stinking old... *brute.*
(and)
My God, I think I'm going to sin.

2.

(Lighting returns.

*FATHER LEW turns up for the appointment at
KISSANE's office.*

*He disguises himself to the degree that he is
wearing a tie rather than his clerical collar.*

*He approaches the open door to the doctor's actual
office with great trepidation. He sees that the
psychiatrist is already in there with OLD MESSY
and, surprisingly, has the old paedophile – quite
illegally -- well under hypnosis.*

*He can see MASSEY is looking far better than his
age would seem. He is not biblically haggard or
transfixed by a lifetime of evil, but lies straight,
even strong, on the couch. In fact, the old boy
emanates a surprising pent-up vigour, as though, in
trance there in a heavy leather chair, he looks as
though he is in his rightful time and place. His
clothes are gaudy, maybe outlandish.*

*His reputed single dahlia is on the table between
him and KISSANE.*

*As FATHER LEW slowly enters, KISSANE motions
silence, waves him to sit down and observe.*

The Poisoning of Old Messy
> *Strangely, KISSANCE is actually humming what
> could well be a lullaby to MASSEY, before nodding
> to the priest that he is about to begin again and:)*

KISSANE: Breathing nice and deeply still. There is only my voice, nothing else, still. You are still smiling looking over at the annexe of the old football pavilion. What do you see over there?"

OLD MESSY: Rubbing the knocks down, yes.

KISSANE: Yes. You said all year round, didn't you? So, there were all sports, many boys you rubbed the knocks down? You can answer.

OLD MESSY: Many, yes.

KISSANE: How many? Alright… many. So now you would like to remember just one of these boys then. I understand. Let's say one of them is the boy you were with a lot. Let's say he is the one they called Skinny. Do you remember him? No? Are you sure? Wasn't he the boy who dared complain and you had expelled for a month? Hmm? Does Skinny ring a bell?

OLD MESSY: No.

KISSANE: Why are you smiling again? Are you smiling because you're lying again?

OLD MESSY: Yes.

KISSANE: Because it feels good?

OLD MESSY: Yes.

KISSANE: Not good so much as nice and familiar…?

OLD MESSY: Yes.

KISSANE: You said there were many.

OLD MESSY: Yes.

KISSANE: Do you remember the boy called Skinny now?

OLD MESSY: Yes.

KISSANE: Breathing easily still. Let's say this skinny lad was here now asking why. What would you say to him?

OLD MESSY: It's just the flesh of it.

KISSANE: Just the flesh of it, you say?

OLD MESSY: Yes.

KISSANE: Is there any form of guilt as you keep breathing nice and easy?

OLD MESSY: No.

KISSANE: No guilt at all?

OLD MESSY: God and the Church is forgiving.

KISSANE: How is that, breathing nice and deeply?

OLD MESSY: You say.

The Poisoning of Old Messy
KISSANE: You mean you ask?

OLD MESSY: No, you say.

KISSANE: (looking at FATHER LEW) You say forgive me and you are forgiven?

OLD MESSY: Yes.

KISSANE: You are feeling nice and safe. You are sleeping deeply. Now, look into the boy called Skinny's eyes. Is God forgiving with him too?

OLD MESSY: (a bit agitated) Dunno.

KISSANE: Ssh, ssh.
    (and)
Who's worse do you think, you or the boy Skinny?

OLD MESSY: The flesh folds into one.

KISSANE: 'The flesh folds into one'? But what if this skinny boy, say, says he hates you? Don't get alarmed. You feel so safe. But what if he just says this because he wants to know why?

OLD MESSY: I would like to sleep now.

KISSANE: But you are sleeping.

OLD MESSY: I would like to sleep now.

KISSANE: Are you saying you would like to escape?

OLD MESSY: Yes.

KISSANE: From the boy Skinny?

OLD MESSY: I need to sleep now.

KISSANE: What if the boy tells you he knows a safe time and all you have to do is close the pavilion's old wooden door behind you...? How would you feel about that?

OLD MESSY: Before the flesh?

KISSANE: Yes, before the flesh folds. How would that be?

OLD MESSY: Okay.

KISSANE: Before having to ask for forgiveness. Before the guilt. Is that how peaceful you want to be? Is that what you're saying to the boy?

OLD MESSY: (acquiescing) Towels, towels. Towels that jump.

KISSANE: Breathe, breathing deeply. Are you sure?

OLD MESSY: Yes.

KISSANE: Then it's time to follow him in to there, do you think?
(the old man seems to hesitate)
Into the old footy pavilion and closing the old wooden door...?

OLD MESSY: Yes.

*(KISSANE looks meaningfully at FATHER LEW
before continuing his session with the old man:)*
191

KISSANE: Yes. If you insist. Breathing deeply. Well, there's his hand in front of you, isn't it? Take his hand there. That's it. Feel how it feels so good, how the flesh folds…? Breathing deeper and deeper. You are already feeling it getting safe, safe, safer. Going back to the old pavilion now. Going back to the old wooden door now. See how you are feeling younger and younger? Yes. See how you nod nice and deeply. See how you are not only feeling but getting younger and younger.

OLD MESSY: (barely a mutter) Yes.

KISSANE: Ssh, ssh now. Getting near now. All warm and wrapping now. No need to nod anymore now. Just follow the boy Skinny's hand. That's right. That's just so good for you. Follow him down. Younger and younger. In the flick of time, in the flesh of time, in the forgiveness of time always given. Hmm? Ummm? Down with the boy. Follow, you follow, he follows. Down, the glade spots. The shade spots. The dark folding spots. Getting younger with the boy Skinny. Still nodding. Still sleeping deeper and deeper. Younger and younger. Holding hands. You are getting younger. Younger. You can't even hold the boy Skinny's hand any longer because see how you can't reach reaching up. The cool and dark spots. Getting smaller and younger. Deeper. Peace. Leaving the boy Skinny behind now. Ten years. Nine years old you are; isn't it so good to feel it? Letting yourself go further down. Just starting school, looking at the nice warm folding flesh. Getting safer, warmer, younger. Yes, and you look and it's your mother's hand now, isn't it? Yes. Oh, yes. And feeling her hands coming over you now, going younger now, two years old now, warm and safe, hmm?, hmm?

OLD MESSY: Ye…

FATHER LEW: (hiss whisper) What are you doing?

(KISSANE casts him a withering look, continues:)

KISSANE: Floating right down now, aren't we? Tiny beats, your little baby heart, so warm and good, now. Where there's beat now. Where there's breath now. Where there's no beat now and there's peace now and that's so good at last now, isn't it? One-two. Feeling how warm you are tucked in her womb now. Warmer, younger, going deeper now. Smaller now. Tinier now. Warmer and safer now. One-two, where there's beat now; there's breath now, no; where there's no beat, there's peace, one-two, one-two and, yes, you are so near at last, aren't you? You want to nod yes but you can't. You don't want to. One. Two. Your heart beats slowing. Slowing now. You are leaving the beats now, warm and blessed. Younger and lovely younger, warm and cosy. Now you are only a few beats old now, the tiny beats now, and now you are blessedly counting them down now. Five, and only tiny beats old now. Four, and the peace, the peace now, warm and blessing. Three and the beats now, Two, and two beats old now. One, and one beat old now. Now comes nothing and there's no beat now. Now there is nothing. Now you are nothing. When I clap my hands twice, you can't wake up. So good to know you will never wake up. Now. Now…

(FATHER LEW rushes over, desperately tries to revive him)

FATHER LEW: He's not breathing!

193

The Poisoning of Old Messy
> *(KISSANE is already at the door and leaving. He is not in the least remorseful. He stops to answer cynically:)*

KISSANE: Oh? What a pity. Don't give up, Father. You never gave up.
> *(and)*

Don't give up, Father. After all, he always got back on his feet when afterwards he called you, right? On the other hand, you could ask his god if the old piece of shit remembers skinny little me now.

(end)

Elegy for a Hanging Carcass

(a stage eloquence for three)

Elegy for a Hanging Carcass

An eloquence for three chanters.

It might be too late for voices to be raised against the life extinctions of the Tasmanian Aborigines and the Tasmanian wolf. But it cannot be too late for voices to be listed elegiacally.

Cast
CHANTER/CANTOR 1
CHANTER/CANTOR 2
CHANTER/CANTOR 3

Setting
The image of the hanging Thylacine… one of the last if
not the last… is projected on a screen and spotlit.

Elegy for a Hanging Carcass

(The image of the hanging Thylacine... one of the last if not the last... is projected on a screen and spotlit.

The rest of the stage remains dark until, eventually, three chanters appear, spread in positions across the front stage. They remain unmoving, are in their own spotlights)

CHANTER 1:
From the photographer's rafter hung the rope hung the
    Thylacine
by the hinders hung near the hunter human-by

CHANTER 2:
hung by the caption 'Extinction is Forever'

CHANTER 3:
hung on the wall, mount-piece. A frame-up.

TOGETHER:
'If one dour opens, another ope-eyes'.

CHANTER 1:
But Truganinni has never known what a joke is in
English, what is forever untranslatable.

CHANTER 2:
Maybe a joke is a better fret than this thing they call
    photograph'd.

199

Elegy for a Hanging Carcass
CHANTER 3:
Extinction, give or take a day.

CHANTER 1:
Still, the old lady frets the fret as it was and is.
The hung carcass where the hunter's eye glints the lens of
        forever
as much as to how forever perpetuated is.

CHANTER 2:
The old lady, now, harrows for its uniquity hung to
        hanging.
She knows in her bones this is the
thin and thane strand of coming to know the hunters…

CHANTER 3:
…in all their suspensions, their scents, their hell bents.
Night sighted, matt-haired reliquary too, she keens and
        keened oh
'Don't let them cut me up!' They did.

CHANTER 1:
Fleshed her out. Strung her bones. Dangled public
        display.

CHANTER 2:
Hung upon a post and psst and ssh-shooting-here. Do
you mind?

CHANTER 3:
                Extinction goes on and on.

        *(They stand immobile for a moment, then solemnly
        change places. When there:)*

CHANTER 2:

The Tasmanian tiger lopes boldly where
humans track on and the moon can candle.

CHANTER 3:
It brings not slink now but is unto the aromas of the sweet
	earths,
the long earths, the ever-bless. Strobes

CHANTER 1:
are its outline as much as the warm mulcts feather its pads
as much is.

CHANTER 2:
Stretches its shoulders, its hips, for this is the night
it has come from for countless generations. Round and
	rounds.

CHANTER 3:
Momentum bounds. No studio affix'd.

CHANTER 1:
The tiger the wolf breaks from wood to clearing
as the moon so candles, gamboling thrall'd
above the ever-lair;

CHANTER 2:
			higher beyond the strange snowlining,
and yoops and yoops down the timelong corridors,
ringing back out the reveilles from all nonhumankinds.

CHANTER 3:
As much as it will come as much is.

CHANTER 1:
The shot too rings out a round and round and round.

Elegy for a Hanging Carcass
Flanked and quivering, it. Hung for the exposures
unending. It ends.

CHANTER 2:
In mind's eye the old lady groans'n'greets at herself
crumpling as well as well is, never understanding:

CHANTER 3:
'Unique forms togetherness form ha ha. You are
the saltpeter of my soul. Simon says peter out'
the hunter jokes or how

TOGETHER:
                                    extinction goes on
and on ever the day

     *(They remain immobile again, then slowly change
     positions once more)*

CHANTER 2:
In the photographic studio, snap,

CHANTER 3:
the wolf the tiger frozen in divebomb hung.

CHANTER 1:
The hunter frozen in esteem.

CHANTER 2:
Still life, rafter-strumped forever.

CHANTER 3:
By the side of a plant stand intimating leaves,

CHANTER 1:
by the side of a weary way, lay-thy-lairy-head,

CHANTER 2:
is borne the light of the extinguishing flames.

CHANTER 3:
Such another thing rung out.

CHANTER 1:
She might not know a joke when she sees it but

CHANTER 2:
old Truganinni there stets how it is the hunters hunt

CHANTER 3:
for the forever of it, for the beaters

CHANTER 1:
she knows are coming over the hill for her too
and yet

CHANTER 2:
     cold and yet uncovered there

CHANTER 3:
did she lay down adoring alone in the alley outside

CHANTER 1:
and sighed aside as much as a dying whimper is...

CHANTER 2:
The joke she would never get was she'd

CHANTER 3:
taken too many pots, shots, and just Schnapps'd

TOGETHER:

203

Elegy for a Hanging Carcass
Outside, just beyond, she was, sure, but extinction's at
    full pelt
They caption'd her Queen.
They caption'd it Thylacine.

CHANTER 1:
But the flashbulb is forever. Exposure; over.

CHANTER 2:
Shot, the days, as much are.

    (They remain stationary for the last time.

    Spots slowly fade)

(end)

The Great Franklin's Blow-up Bottles

(from 'The 1001 Lankan Nights', a tattle tale for pipsqueaks)

One act tattle tale of a fable for pipsqueaks from 'The 1001 Lankan Nights'.

The Troubadour is back around the campfire relating from the Talls chronicles of the ages how far greater than any ordinary mesmerist is The Great Franklin. The tale is told as to how, in one instance, The Great Franklin can wreak terrible vengeance when 'his foible is foib'd', yet, in the next instance, he can be so lovingly helpful to Tiny Nita – a child who before The Great Franklin came along had stopped growing at the age of four but who, after The Great Franklin had left, could turn out (but sweetly!) as a Sumo wrestler at the age of fourteen.

Cast
TROUBADOUR
THE GREAT FRANKLIN
TINY NITA
Her mother

various, to mill around as shadow party goers

Setting
The troubadour sits at a campfire. Behind him, projected
onto a screen or the backdrop. sparks fly into the night.

The Great Franklin's Blow-up Bottles

(It is yarn telling time, and the shadows projected on that screen behind him reflect his dancing story telling:)

TROUBADOUR: In this lubbery Talls retelling time when all the shaggy dogs wag their tales blowing their woosh-woosh pull-this-ones as sparks into literature's thin atmosphere, there was none known better or worse than the great hypnotist The Great Franklin. No, there wasn't. He was so great, they called him a hypnotist because when it came to eye power he shot from the hyp. He did. There was no denying that, even if there was.

(and)

The Great Franklin was also the magician you so often saw at those kids' birthday parties. Oh, you may ask why would such a great man bother with so many kids' birthday parties? This is what I'm here for, to tell you why. It was because The Great Franklin's one weakness was he would do anything for crumbs. Yes, crumbs! When it came to crumbs, especially any last crumb, those famous eyes of his were ogles, those fingers that controlled whole chunky masses of the world, quivering messes. It was true. The Great Franklin quivered among any crumby mess. Didn't sparks fly then!

(and)

I almost said The Great Franklin quivered unbested among any crumby mess. But as incredible as it might seem that was not quite true. There was one time of the

209

The Great Franklin's Blow-up Bottles

Talls once-upon-a-time that the great man was left quivering among the crumby mess.

(and)

Those of you who have sat around this fire, this can't-believe-your-ears, may have already heard-Talls-tell that that time was the time of the sixth birthday bash of the Sliding-Tits Twins, ruffian and rogue sons of a top politician who slid over for no one, except for each other when confronted by a milk tit. And that wasn't too often since weaning. But the real trouble was no birthday cake was good enough for these two terrible twins; they just loved the crumbs too. They did. Like The Great Franklin himself, they would just do anything for the crumbs. They went to other kids' birthday parties with plastic hammers and, if you were not careful, they would smash that precious cake of yours to smithereen crumbs and then horridly and big-bullingly fall upon them!

(and)

And so, as the Talls retelling of it has it, in front of The Great Franklin himself, let alone all their guests, the Sliding-Tit Twins smashed to pieces their own birthday cake and gluttonously consume every last crumb for themselves, their bodyguards with weapons drawn in a protective circle around them included. Well, the chronicles that tattle down the centuries do not need to tell you of The Great Franklin's horror and disgust at having those crumbs, so near and yet so dire'd, gobbled up before his very famous eyes.

(and)

Don't think The Great Franklin merely settled his wrath on the twins. His wrath-making genius was far broader than that. It took in the whole gathering there, the complicit other six-year-olds there at the party who stood back and watched and the mothers who had stood back and laughed as the Sliding-Tit Twins consumed every last crumb-drop.

210

(pointing up to the shadow play)
Just look at the Sliding-Tit twins go up there.

(He has to wait impatiently while the twins hog all the crumbs. Finally, he can continue)

TROUBADOUR: Hogs. You know, I hate that bit. They are the only two six-year-olds I know who don't care a hoot about holding up a good yarn. Thankfully, the well-pull-this-one retelling allows me to put in a good 'though' here...
(carries on)
Now, there was one and her mother there, 'though', who The Great Franklin did not include in his revenge and retribution... a little stunted child who was born as a cousin to the Sliding-Tit Twins at the very same instant, but who had been so squeezed out by them bullying elbowing her aside that she had stopped growing at the age of four. Her name was Tiny Nita. It was, and what a little dear! What a tiny little love! What a lot of great heart did The Great Franklin's heart put out to her! Oh, they had tests. They had sent her overseas to three African cities to be stretched by association with tall African warriors by the neck up and by the neck down. They put little lead shoes on her feet and two helium balloons to each shoulder. But nothing worked and nothing was found that could explain why, except what was obvious to everyone: she had just gotten squeezed between the births of her two hateful crumb-devouring thriving twin cousins, that's all. Nothing medically could be done about it now. It was Nature showing its sharp hie-thee elbows and, when looked back on, hindsight going all blunt on it. But, oh, what a living doll!
(and)
Even so, our great man could not stop being our great man. Even under such fire, the Great Franklin could never

The Great Franklin's Blow-up Bottles

stop being the Great Franklin, however battered or
bruised by crumb-deprivation he might be. Watching
those two crumby twins gutsing themselves made the
Great Franklin flamin' mad. He stood to his full fearsome
height, as amid the throng he was wont to do, and he
waved... yes, instantly... for all (except Tiny Nita and her
mother!) there to shut their cakeholes. He did. And
didn't he then let loose those famous hypnotic eyes upon
them all going in full-throttled English as it is spoken:

> *(THE GREAT FRANKLIN steps forward in all his
> kid's-party magician's outfit. He is in booming
> control; his eyes are (literally) lasers. All projected
> back in the shadow play fall down or sway before
> him...)*

GREAT FRANKLIN: Listen up, kiddies and mumsicals.
Golly gosh, aren't we all feeling sleepy. Sleepy byes.
That's it, good night. Nightie night nice and cosy. There
you go. But, gulp!, you haven't touched all that beaut-
eyed ice cream on the table in front of you where the best
of crumbs used to be! Horror! And all that strawberry,
blueberry, choccy, vanilla ice cream going to waste while
you're all holding back! Oh, lick, lick. Tongues out, lick
lick. But as much as we lick-lick our tongues out, we
cannot reach the ice creamy-weamy, can we? We all
know why, don't we? Nod our heads. Lick-lick. That's
right; it's because you know that if your tongues, lick-
lick, ever reach the ice cream, it will disappear forever.
Oh, no! But it will! If your tongues ever get to take a
lick-lick touch that ice cream, that ice cream, like all ice
cream forevermore, will disappear from your lives! Not
just now but, yes, for always! Oh, dear! Oh, how awful!
Oh, how terrible for you! No more ice cream, ever! How
you crave just a little lick! Put your tongue out for that
lick-lick. That's it. But, oh dear, when you do, that ice

cream jumps further away threatening not to stop going away, not to stop, threatening never to come back! No, don't cry. You can only go lick-lick when you think of the ice cream you will never have again, but what to do? What to do? You can only try lick-lick harder. And harder. And harder. While the ice cream is going, going... gone! Gone forever now! Oh, it's such a crying shame, isn't it?'

TROUBADOUR: And what a shocking sight to behold! What a terrible Talls-retelling priced to pay for depriving the great man of crumbs... having to poke your tongue out and lick-lick whenever you come across ice cream knowing you will never be able to get near any ice cream again.
    (and)
Smoke curls of 'well-would-you-ever!' swill into the full-moon's lux, with luck.
    (carries on)
Except... and ever great story has an 'except'... The Great Franklin had avoided including little Tiny Nita and her mother, hadn't he? Besides, the poor little love was too delicate or too crushed by one of her constant migraines migraine to be caught up in the lick-lick carnage. Indeed The Great Franklin carried her imaginary portion of imaginary ice cream... the little dear imagined she liked the vanilla best ... over to her and let her daintily nibble at it under her mum's permission until she was full, her eyes star-bright with pleasure at last... a little respite from her headaches... until he kissed the top of her little fair head.

(and as the shadow play would have it:)

TROUBADOUR: And then did The Great Franklin leave the party. It is recorded as possibility the first time he

213

The Great Franklin's Blow-up Bottles
ever kneed two six-year-old twins in the crutch as he
went. Not with such precise anatomical targetry. He
comforted himself, as the story goes, that even great men
have their ups and downs, have their foibles foib'd.

(waits as necessary, before:)

TROUBADOUR: But, soft! You must be tired in this
dreamy haze of the Talls retelling campfire. Let me give
you a rest while the scene is changed to 'scene 2: the
grotto' before your very eyes. It is a shady grotto you
could hardly credit would appear out of seeming nowhere
somewhere between the tongues going a-lickin' and the
front gate…

2.

*(The grotto, where TINY NITA and her mother are
sitting looking up at the GREAT FRANKLIN.*

*Projected on the backdrop is the more metaphysical
situation… where TINY NITA nestles so easily in
the crook of her mother's arms… and grows bigger
and bigger as the Talls tale develops:)*

TROUBADOUR: The grotto. Ah. Don't we all say 'Ah'
when we see a grotto? What the Great Franklin sees is
how the mother has somehow (oh, the magic of it!) has
brought Little Nita there and how he has found his great
self sitting so greatly next to them. A mite so miniature.
The tiny little tot is nestled in her mother's hand, and,
oh… and don't we always say 'oh' when we hear it?… has
such a throbbing headache. Oh and oh… And the Great
Franklin has such love in his great heart for the tiniest of
tots, so softly.

(and)

And so, kiddikins, here beginneth the tattle tale of 'The
Bottles Not Big Enough for the Dear Little Thing'…

(He flourishes for:)

GREAT FRANKLIN: I know why you're here, Nita, little
Nita.

TINY NITA: (smallest of voices) Why?

GREAT FRANKLIN: Ah, your poor little headaches so
much.

TINY NITA: Why?

GREAT FRANKLING: It's just the lack of growing, you
see.

TINY NITA: Why?

GREAT FRANKLIN: It's only because you live in a jar.

TINY NITA: Do I?

GREAT FRANKLIN: You do, and it keeps rattling you
around and giving you a headache.

TINY NITA: Yes.

GREAT FRANKLIN: I had another friend like that.
Hers was a peanut-butter jar, a bit bigger than yours, but
she was a bit fuller than you. Her name was Picaninny.
What's your jar?

TINY NITA: Don't know.

GREAT FRANKLIN: Personally, I think it's a marmalade jam jar, an orange marmalade jam jar.

TINY NITA: Yes.

GREAT FRANKLIN: My friend Picaninny got rattled in the peanut-butter jar she lived in, too, and she got headaches like you, too. She was a lively little girl just like you, too.

TINY NITA: How?

GREAT FRANKLIN: She had springs in her step just like you, don't you think?

TINY NITA: (eyes so large) I don't know.

GREAT FRANKLIN: Yes, you do, silly. Springs in your steps, springs in your feet. I've seen. Now, I'll tell you something about that just between you and I and your mother, of course.

TINY NITA: Please.

GREAT FRANKLIN: In that peanut-butter jar and with all that spring in her step, it was a real trouble Picaninny too, you see. She kept springing upwards in that jar and she kept hitting her head on the lid. She did! It kept making it hurt; it kept making it throb, giving it a terrible headache all the time because she didn't have anything to stop her head from hitting the top of the jar whenever she tried to spring upwards. That was why Picaninny sometimes cried. It wasn't because of all the nasty things they said about her size like everyone thought. It was because she couldn't use the spring in her steps without hurting her head and giving herself a headache. Like you.

TINY NITA: Yes.

GREAT FRANKLIN: But do you know what happened to tears when you live in a jar like Picaninny's peanut butter jar and like your orange marmalade jar?

TINY NITA: No.

GREAT FRANKLIN: Are you nestling comfortably in your mother's arms there?

(The projection on the backdrop shows her to be doing so, but perceptibly bigger even yet)

TINY NITA: Yes.

GREAT FRANKLIN: Well, in that case, I can tell you Picaninny came to know what happened to the tears hitting her head all the time on the top of her peanut jar. She did. One day she looked down and saw that her tears had made a crocodile in a pool on the bottom of her jar. Not that she was too surprised; she knew that crocodiles come from tears. She also knew how crocodiles were strong. She knew they didn't like living at the bottom of jars under little girls' feet because crocodiles were too springy for any of that. They were so springy, they even put them on to wear as shoes. So you know what happened? Picaninny, she rocked and rocked her peanut butter jar until it tipped over. She upped and did! Now, it gave her a bit of that headache again, but, when it did topple over, the crocodile swam to the top up by the lid and when that happened Picaninny quickly rocked and rattled her jar again so that it popped back upright again.

217

And there it was. She had the top of her head covered by a crocodile and she had done all that by herself by thinking things through.

(He waits through the questioning silence)
‘

GREAT FRANKLIN: After that Picaninny used and used the spring in her step as much as she liked without hurting herself because her head only hit the soft belly of Mr Crocodile. Yes, and she kept this up until all those natural springs she had inside her made her become so much bigger -- until that one day the top of the jar just had to fly off to make room for her. Well! She looked down and saw the reason for that was she had simply outgrown the jar and hadn't realised it all that time. How about that?!
(pointing up to the screen)
Can you see how much she is growing on the grotto wall?

TINY NITA: (nodding) Oh.

GREAT FRANKLIN: That growing too big for the jar was what really was hurting the top of her head, you see. That was what was giving her the headache all the time. She'd been just too big for the jar all along. She just hadn't realised it.
(and)
When you cry, do you make a crocodile at the bottom of your orange marmalade jar?

TINY NITA: Yes.

GREAT FRANKLIN: I'm sure you do too! Well then, you know what to do. You use all that spring you have to your feet and you rock and rock and you tip the jar up and you tip it over on its head and then you tip it back and... see...

(pointing up to the shadow play),
Mr Crocodile is not under your feet anymore but on your
head like a great big cushion and you can spring up as
much as you like without hitting your head or getting a
headache until that old top just flies off to make room for
you, and how much you've grown.

TINY NITA: Yes.

TROUBADOUR: (breaking in) The tiny little thing was
looking at him with so much hope it filled her eyes, but
still her tears came so large for such a tiny face that the
Great Franklin's chest hurt and his famous eyes had to
drop. 'Oh dear, why are you crying?', he asked.

MOTHER: (weepily) Because Mr Crocodile won't swim
up to the top for her and no matter how much she jumps
and jumps she keeps hurting her head and the headache
won't stop.

GREAT FRANKLIN: Well, little wonder.
(to the little girl)
Just look at those feet of yours.

TINY NITA: Why?

GREAT FRANKLIN: Can you point your toes upwards?

TINY NITA: (trying) No.

GREAT FRANKLIN: Can you bend your foot towards
the sky?

TINY NITA: No.

GREAT FRANKLIN: Of course you can't. You've got your crocodile on backwards, silly. How can Mr Crocodile swim to the top of your jar when he can't even see where he's going?

TINY NITA: Oh.

GREAT FRANKLIN: So what do you do about that? I'll tell you what Picaninny did. She used the spring in her step to turn her feet around the right way and it didn't take a minute.

TINY NITA: Did she?

GREAT FRANKLIN: You try it.

(She does as shown on the shadow play)

TROUBADOUR: She did. Little Tiny Nita used the spring in her legs to turn her feet around the right way, all the time looking now up at her mother with no-tiny joy in her eyes, look I can do it.

TINY NITA: See?

MOTHER: (tearfully) Yes.

GREAT FRANKLIN: What's that old crocodile doing now?

TINY NITA: (daring to feel happy) The naughty old thing is swimming past my nose.

GREAT FRANKLIN: And where's he going?

TINY NITA: To the top of my head so I can bounce and bounce and it doesn't hurt.

GREAT FRANKLIN: What doesn't hurt, silly?

TINY NITA: What...

> *(her little neck having to crick a bit so she can still fit beneath her mother's armpit which she had never been able to even reach up and touch before)*

TINY NITA: ...my friends say about me not growing.

GREAT FRANKLIN: That's right! Now we're getting somewhere! It was the same with my friend Picaninny, what with her head not hurting because Mr Crocodile was up there and Mr Crocodile didn't give a fig for what her friends said about her not growing. Now, do you want to know what Picaninny did next?

TINY NITA: Yes.

GREAT FRANKLIN: My friend Picaninny was so happy about not being hurt by what her friends said about her being so small, she just kept on bouncing and bouncing until she popped out of that peanut butter jar because she was certainly just too big for it now with all that springing going on in her steps.
>   *(and)*
So they had to get her a new home. They did! The peanut jar was too small for her now! And this new home was a Heinz tomato sauce bottle, much bigger and not so fat as the old peanut jar, so she didn't rattle around from side to side so much, and her mother only had to put a paper tissue in the top to keep the flies off because she knew that, with those springs in Picaninny's steps now,

no proper top was going to hold her down for much
longer or hold her in anyway.
        (and)
Do you think that might have been the end of that?

TINY NITA: No.

GREAT FRANKLIN: How right you are! Next, after
she had soon grown right out of the Heinz sauce bottle,
they had to get a great big Jeroboam bottle to fit her. A
Jeroboam bottle was a great big bottle for the finest of
wines. But with all those springs in her steps, soon the
Jeroboam bottle wasn't big enough for Picaninny either.
Oh dear, oh dear, they went... this little girl's springing up
so fast!

MOTHER: 'This little girl's springing up so fast!"

GREAT FRANKLIN: Too right she was! So then they
had to look for bigger and bigger bottles of the finest
wines, up and up in size, pouring her out of one and into
the other, until they could only fit her into the biggest
bottle of all. A Melchidezek, they called it, and that
bottle-new-home so tall they put a candle on it so planes
didn't fly into it, so ships knew it was there and cars could
go around it. But also they put a candle on it to light the
way onwards and upwards for children who weren't as
grown up as Picaninny was now either. Would you
believe that?

TINY NITA: Yes.

GREAT FRANKLIN: You are saying yes, but I think
you know that wasn't the real secret as to why Picaninny
grew, was it?

TINY NITA: I don't think so

GREAT FRANKLIN: No. And how right you are! You see, Mr Crocodile had given her a secret word because Mr Crocodile knew how much she would grow with all those springs in her step and how she would need something extra when she had grown to a certain size. And with that secret word, all Picaninny had to do was look up to the candle on the top of her bottle and say that word and then pull herself up on the rope that would fall down from the sky for her to climb up on...
(teasingly)
What are you wearing that little frown for? I suppose that big sticky-beak of a little nose of yours wants to know that secret word.

TINY NITA: Yes, please.

GREAT FRANKLIN: You have to promise not to tell.

TINY NITA: I promise.

GREAT FRANKLIN: Well, I suppose it's all right since your name is Nita, or I trust it is. Listen. You listening? Ssh, ssh, that secret magic word is... Eeny-meeny. With a hyphen so it's only one word.

TINY NITA: Eeny-meeny.

GREAT FRANKLIN: Eeny-meeny with a hyphen, only one word.

TINY NITA: Eeny-meeny.

GREAT FRANKLIN: Sssh. Not so loud or it won't be secret word. And when Picaninny pulled on that rope that

The Great Franklin's Blow-up Bottles
fell from the sky as soon as she said that secret word,
what do you think happened to her head and shoulders?

TINY NITA: What?

GREAT FRANKLIN: They rose, silly.

TINY NITA: What did?

GREAT FRANKLIN: Her head and shoulders, what
else? They did, taking her with them. And nobody ever
saw her head and shoulders again, not from above, they
didn't... not unless they were flying on a horse with
wings or something.

> *(TINY NITA giggles with glee. As shown in the
> shadow play, she has been growing until, now, she
> is up to having head bent just to tuck it under the
> chin of her mother – while the heels of her feet with
> all that spring in them are tapping way beyond her
> mother's knees 'way down there' now)*

GREAT FRANKLING: (clapping hands) I think you're
growing too big already!

TINY NITA: I am!

GREAT FRANKLIN: I think you think you're just like
my friend Picaninny.

TINY NITA: I am!

GREAT FRANKLIN: With the spring in your feet and
your own Mr Crocodile.

TINY NITA: Yes!

GREAT FRANKLIN: You know what happened to Mr Crocodile, don't you?

TINY NITA: (stopping) No.

> *(But her head in the shadow play has now gone past her mother's head and, in there, she is curiously looking down on the top of her mother's head, so large is she getting)*

GREAT FRANKLIN: Are you sure?

TINY NITA: Yes.

GREAT FRANKLIN: What a pity! I was hoping you could tell me… only as a secret, mind.

TINY NITA: Sorry.

GREAT FRANKLIN: Well, what is distracting you?

TINY NITA: I don't know.

GREAT FRANKLIN: Of course you know. You looking down on the top of your mother's head because you've never seen it before. Nobody has seen the top of her head before, isn't that right? It's like your head and shoulders. You'd have to be flying on a horse with wings to be able to look down on them, wouldn't you.

TINY NITA: (delighted) Yes!

GREAT FRANKLIN: Why's that?

TINY NITA: Because I'm growing so much!

225

The Great Franklin's Blow-up Bottles

GREAT FRANKLIN: You know what I think?

TINY NITA: What?

GREAT FRANKLIN: This grotto ain't big enough for both you and me.

TINY NITA: (giggling) No.

GREAT FRANKLIN: So do you wanna go back into the party and knock a few heads together?

TINY NITA: Yes!

GREAT FRANKLIN: Just be a bit careful you don't trip over all the tongues hanging out near where the ice cream is.

TINY NITA: (childish punching movements) Pow! Pow!

> *(By now, the shadow play has her so large, she has her feet on the ground and is flopped over her standing mother's shoulder. Her shadow can hardly fit on the screen any longer.*
>
> *Blackout, leaving only TROUBADOUR sitting by the campfire again)*

TROUBADOUR: As the chronicles of good-old-yarns has the Talls retelling of it, The Great Franklin did not return to the party but made a great escape before the powerful-politician father of the Sliding-Tit Twins returned home. But Tiny Nita and her mother did. The dear little not-so-little love was already back inside the birthday party and getting her rightful share of it, you bet. Her twin cousins, pipsqueaks really, she found, were already finding out from a little cousin lady of their own size for a change what it was like to get the squeeze put on, to get the boot put in, to be squeezed and boot-up-the-quoited out… with a fair bit of catch-up pinching along the way. Squawk or squeeze on this, either way, you Sliding-Tit Twins!, did little Tiny Nita go – and she never looked back!

(As the spotlight fading from him)

TROUBADOUR: There you go then, as the sparks fly. See, how your ears can fib-flap and your cheeks fib-burn when the Talls-retells how a great man can wreak terrible vengeance when 'his foible is foib'd', yet, in the next instance, be so lovingly helpful to a child like Tiny Nita – a child who before The Great Franklin had stopped growing at the age of four but who, after The Great Franklin, could turn out (but sweetly!) as a Sumo wrestler at the age of fourteen.

(end)